do I get a happy ending?

Valentin Mings

NEWMAN SPRINGS PUBLISHING
320 Broad Street
Red Bank, NJ 07701

First originally published by Newman Springs Publishing 2024

This book discusses sensitive material, including but not limited to sexual assault, suicidal ideation, death, abusive situations, body image, religion, violence, and more.

ISBN 978-1-68498-849-5 (Paperback)
ISBN 978-1-68498-850-1 (Digital)

Printed in the United States of America

Preface

When I started writing this book, I was sitting in a metaphysical weight of my depression and anxiety surrounding my life. I was failing my classes and didn't really have any friends at my job yet. I was new to a city and wasn't getting along with my roommates, and my friends that already lived here didn't have time to see me. I was sitting at my desk, and I had the sudden thought, *How the fuck did I get here?*

So I decided to write about my life. For the protection and privacy of everyone involved, I excluded all names and changed genders and details and locations of events, without affecting the integrity of any situation. I resolved that I was going to take the time and map out how I got to be where I am. Soon after telling my therapist about this book I was writing, he asked me how it ended.

"What does your ending look like? Do you get a happy ending?"

At the time, I didn't have an answer for him. Shortly after I started writing, Misha Collins's poetry book, *Some Things I Still Can't Tell You*, came out. An absolutely beautiful collection of poetry and thought-provoking writing that ultimately made me realize I also didn't want to feel like that. I don't want to leave a situation, to leave this earth, and realize that I've left so many important things unsaid. So this became a memoir of sorts, everything I didn't say at the time that I wish I had, all my thoughts and feelings that I left unprocessed for so long. It was draining to unpack them after all this time.

This is my story. This is my life. This is for everyone who has passed through my life, everyone still in it, and everyone I will meet in the future. This is my soul.

This is my path to a happy ending.

--

"I think I was five. No, four. Four and five, it was my fifth birthday. I was a princess. Well, I was dressed as a princess, everyone was. It was a princess party. I had two cakes; one was a smiley face, but I can't remember what the other one was. Why did I have two cakes anyways? Whatever, that's not important. I was really excited for a neighborhood boy to come. I don't think I liked him. He was in high school, but I did look up to him, I guess. Anyways, I guess that's my earliest memory, everything after that is blurry until middle school, unless I really focus. Is that normal?" I pause and look at him, waiting for validation or an easy answer. Anything to make me feel, well, normal. His eyes are gentle, amused, concerned.

"Is that a good memory?"

I twist my bracelet around my arm.

"Yeah, I guess. It's good. I was having fun." Fun. When was the last time I had fun? When was the last time I went outside? This appointment is the only reason I've even left my room recently. That's not good. "I don't do that many fun things anymore."

"Why do you think that is?"

"I have no one to do fun things with anymore," I say. "My best friend lives almost three hours away, and everything costs money, money I don't have." Everyone said the transition into college life away from home would be hard, and I thought I had a handle on it. I thought I could do it. I keep remembering what my ex said as we drove across the state line: "You can't plan life," they said.

"I couldn't plan life. I have no idea what I'm doing." It's hard to admit it. They were right. I tried my best, but I'm at the wrong school. The wrong school in the wrong city with the wrong job with the wrong people. Sure, I actually have friends at this school; and yes,

I'm studying the right thing. Still, it's just all wrong. I'm burning out. I've burnt out. How did that little princess with two birthday cakes turn into me?

When I was a child, I resented that I had a winter birthday. I always wanted to have a pool party, like my brother, but never could. It was too cold to go swimming or play outside. While I understood the logic of that, I never liked it. It was one month after Christmas, slightly too close to Valentine's Day. For some reason, I always thought Christmas and my birthday would merge into each other, that, eventually, they'd be celebrated as one event. It had never been suggested that something like that would happen. I just always assumed it would. It was almost like I wanted these bad things to happen to me. Of course, I wanted to be liked and loved and to be friends with everyone, but I also wanted bad things to happen so I could act like something was wrong until someone noticed and asked about it. I suppose I craved some kind of attention. I'm not sure why. Maybe I felt ignored, tucked away into a box to be dealt with later.

The most embarrassing day of my life, so far, was in fourth grade. I was ignored that day. I felt sick, really, terribly sick. I was at an after-school workshop, and we had just gotten up from our desks to walk around or go to the bathroom. Minutes after we got back, I felt it. I needed to throw up. Bad.

Naturally, I raised my hand. I was being ignored by the teacher, which isn't unusual, even to this day. However, the consequences were horrifying. I waved my hand. I bounced up and down. I pointed. I tried to get someone else's attention. Until finally, my lips couldn't stay closed anymore. I still feel so terrible for that poor soul who was next to me. I puked, on them, on me, on the floor, the table. I also started sobbing. That was the worst day. For some reason, from that day forward, I threw up every year, every single year like clockwork, around March, until my senior year of high school.

In eighth grade, it was so bad that I couldn't even walk up the stairs to class. I'd go up the stairs for class, get sick, go down to the office, get sick, go back up to class, get sick, go down for lunch or another class, get sick. I had to get an elevator pass just to avoid that. This boy I was "dating" rode the elevator with me. I wasn't necessarily scared of elevators; I just didn't like them much. I told him all of this. I asked him to not do anything stupid. But once in the elevator, he immediately jumped. We didn't break up for another few months. I was in love.

I know how crazy that sounds. A middle schooler? In love? Yes. Love. Love means something different to me now than it did then. My understanding and definition of the word has changed and matured as I have changed and matured. I've heard people say something along the lines of "I thought I was in love, but I didn't know what love was."

I've even said that a few times. Then I realized, I knew what love was. Love to me in middle school was just as real, just as intense, just as deep as love is to me now. The only difference is that now, I can feel more intensely, deeper, more passionately. Love now isn't crying about missing each other or kissing to make up after an argument. Love is understanding boundaries and respecting them. It's being able to talk about disagreements calmly and rationally without fighting. It's sitting next to each other in silence without any awkward tension in the air.

"Sometimes I'm afraid I won't find love," I say. Wait. That's not what I mean. "Well, no, I know I can find love and fall in love even. I guess I'm afraid I won't be able to maintain a healthy relationship with anyone, ever." Really, I'm afraid of getting hurt again.

I wait for an answer, but there isn't one. I open my eyes to see my ceiling staring back at me. I lost myself in my subconscious. I like to plan out conversations before I have them, something about feeling like if I say the wrong thing, I'll lose all my friends. Dramatic. I know. But this time, I hit a problem I can't subconsciously solve for myself. I close my eyes.

"If I can't tell people the parts of myself I'm most ashamed of, how will anyone know me intimately enough to spend their life with me? To love me?"

I can't even admit some of these things to myself. I guess that's why I pretend. Avoiding responsibility is so much easier than owning it and trying to convince everyone I've grown from it. Even if I have.

"People don't change," they say. But sometimes, sometimes they do. Shouldn't they be given a chance to show that they have changed? Do they deserve that chance in the first place?

--

The day I realized that not every girl sometimes pretends to be a boy, I was already pretty sure I was nonbinary. I was eighteen, and I always joked about being called "sir" by some of the younger boys at work. When it started to feel better than being called "ma'am," I didn't pay that much attention to it. When someone told me that he wanted a dick, my first response was "Yeah, me too sometimes."

"What? No. You don't. I want one to, like, piss out of and just have all the time."

"Oh, yeah. I guess I don't want that," I said. But I did, sometimes.

"Yeah. I know. You don't understand." I understood enough.

I didn't know I was nonbinary until a few months after that. I didn't even consider it until I stopped talking to him. I wanted to be a lesbian. I thought in order to be a lesbian, I had to be a girl. I thought I had to be a lesbian to like girls. Neither is true. On some level, I knew I wasn't a girl, and I had the right words to describe how I felt. But I didn't use them. I thought those words weren't for me, which, in hindsight, doesn't make any sense. Of course, I could use these words, if they applied to me, and they did. Figuring out I wasn't a girl, or a boy, was freeing, in some ways, at least.

I would no longer have to conform to societal ideas of femininity and womanhood. I wouldn't have to act super masculine either. I could just exist in the way that feels right to me. The problem was, I didn't know what way felt right. I still don't. It's all very confusing, trying to succeed at mundane day-to-day activities while figuring out how I'm supposed to interact with the world around me, figuring out how to be confident in myself when society doesn't accommodate for my existence. It's weird. It feels amazing. It's also alienating, isolating, difficult. It's freeing, wonderful, exciting. I don't know what I'm doing.

--

I get so emotional sometimes. For about three years, once every few months, I would get a chocolate cheesecake from the Cheesecake Factory and put on Titanic, the one with Kate Winslet, and I would eat and cry and cry and eat and eat and cry until my eyes got puffy. At least, I thought they were puffy. I didn't know what it truly meant to have puffy, after-crying eyes until I got dumped and cried for nearly eight straight hours. It hurt to even open my eyes after that.

Now little things make me cry. I was watching a dance competition while at work, and these high school dance teams were doing such a good job I couldn't help but cry. I love *Criminal Minds*, but those opening scenes—the ones that simply introduce the case—began making me sob.

These poor people! I'd think. *They have no idea what's coming for them!* What's worse, however, is I would immediately berate myself for crying. *Of course, these people know what's happening. This is a television show! These people literally auditioned to be killed in the opening scene!* Naturally, criticizing myself for being upset only made me more upset, made me cry more. Obviously, I know it's a show! I know it's scripted! So why do I get so swept up and invested in it all? Why is it so hard to pull myself completely back into reality?

I know how that sounds, but believe me, I don't confuse reality with fiction. I just get really, deeply involved with stories and universes that aren't mine. I recently binged this show that consistently talks about magic. I love magic and the notion that there's something more to this world than what meets the eye. Fairies, witches, wizards, ghosts—it's all so exciting. I'm captivated by these false narratives, these romanticized versions of life. Yes, there's pain. Yes, people suffer. Yes, it's imperfect. But the inclusion of something otherworldly, something mythical or mystical, makes it all seem worth it.

If I could, I'd spend all my days searching for that something. I would go everywhere, try everything, do whatever I could to see sparks fly out of my fingertips, to feel a god or goddess speak to me, to feel God speak to me. Where is God? Why is it so lonely in the real world? What is God, the person, the thing that created everything! All these stars, all these planets, all this universe! Are we really supposed to believe this is all there is? There must be magic somewhere. Small magics are everywhere. Everyone has magic in them. For example, I can always pop a perfect bag of popcorn. It's my own personal magic, which is fantastic. It's beautiful in its own way. Yet I crave something more, something bigger. I crave magic that can be noticed by other people. I crave fiction.

Where did this craving for magic start? Did I watch too much Disney as a child? Read too many stories about fairies and witches? Or did I watch and read those things because I craved magic deep inside me? A classic "which came first" conundrum. The craving or the content?

--

I've been depressed lately, nothing too dramatic, just sitting in the bedroom of my uni apartment, in my bed, day after day, wishing I could get up and do something but not having the energy to, not even caring to try. It sucks, a lot, because honestly I want to do stuff. I want to go to class and see my friends and live my life, but I can't just do it. No matter what I try, the incentives, the fun, the joy, nothing works.

One of the actors in the show I just started bingeing has quickly become my favorite. I have the *biggest* platonic crush on that man. It's a little ridiculous. I admit. There's just something about his voice that is really, really calming and comforting to me. I want a video of him telling me that I can do anything and that I'll be okay and all that good stuff, maybe even saying he's proud of me, although that feels a bit extreme. My best friend thinks it's a little ridiculous that I'm so infatuated with him, but I think that says more about him than it does about me, especially since it's not infatuation but admiration. He's like my emotional-support-actor guy, like someone I can look up to, I guess.

Finding comfort and peace in odd places is important to living, I think. You can find joy in things like the wind blowing through the trees or the sound of a child laughing, but joy is different than peace. Peace is quiet, calm, safe. Joy is exciting, butterflies in the stomach, sounds like laughter. I love joy, and even though I haven't felt it in a while, I remember it clearly. Watching the show provides me with a sense of peace and comfort. Maybe I'm content. Is happiness the same thing as contentment? Maybe I can't tell what happiness is anymore. Does that happen to people, or do people get so used to being content and peaceful that they can't tell what happiness is again? I don't think so. I hope not.

I was unhappy when I went to a different school for only one grade, in the middle of elementary school. My parents thought it'd be a better opportunity, but it was very uncomfortable to be transferred to a new school and a new class and a new place just two weeks into the school year. Everyone knew each other already. Everyone had friends already. I felt alone. I had to wear a skirt, and I hated it. Uniforms have never really been my thing. Eventually, after weeks of complaining to my mom, I was able to wear pants instead of a skirt. I wore jeans and pants every day from that point forward until I got comfortable with my body again. No, that's not true. Until I put my worth in my ability to be sexualized by the male gaze and wrapped it up in "body positivity" and "self-love." I still don't fully love my body, but that's more dysphoria than anything else.

I started picking at my skin that year. I wouldn't create wounds or scratches, at least not intentionally, just pick at bug bites or scrapes from falling. Any imperfections I found on my body fell victim to my fingernails, even moles, which were especially frustrating because I couldn't do anything about them. My parents tried scare tactics to make me want to stop, but they never worked. I suppose showing me pictures of people with giant welts and raw areas on their body had the opposite reaction than the one they were hoping for. I got more upset and stressed, so I would pick at myself more. It was self-harm. I never thought of it as self-harm, and I suppose they didn't either. Although I was quite literally harming myself, it wasn't cutting or burning or breaking my bones. It was all so easy to hide then, and even easier now, although I don't do it nearly as often as I used to. Was this also my need for attention? I don't know.

What I do know is it made me feel better, more in control maybe. When I couldn't do anything about a situation that made me feel bad, I could do something about how I showed that I was affected. I never wanted to cause a scene, make a bad impression, draw too much negative attention. I always did what I was told and hardly ever acted out poorly. I didn't want to be another negative in my parents' life, cause another argument or yelling match in the living room. I put this insane amount of pressure on myself to be perfect or as close to perfect as I could muster. I did well in school and made friends. Though, I've never had a lot of them, and when I had more than one, I'd be the one left behind. I'd walk behind the group when the sidewalk was too small. I'd be told about gatherings when it was too late for me to get permission to go. I had a best friend that school year. I don't remember her name. She made me feel not so alone, like I had a place I belonged. I still appreciate her.

I was always searching for some place to belong. I still am. It's difficult not fitting in with any friend group. I grew up in church. It was very segregated. Everyone knew everyone, but distinct friend groups were made and hard to join. The groups interacted (I mean it was church), and we were all friends on some shallow level. Still, I didn't feel right with them, any of them. I had my best friends, we still talk, but also some emptiness that couldn't be satisfied. I was waiting for the Lord to fill that hole, and that's not what happened. I had few friends at school, no real friends. I had a best friend in first grade, who basically started drama with a neighborhood girl I befriended, then yelled at me when I didn't want to be friends with her anymore.

"It's because of that other girl, isn't it?" she screamed.

"No, you're just not being very nice. You lied about her," I told her.

"I never lied about her! She's the worst! You're the worst! I hate you!" she cried.

Talk about drama. To make matters worse, the other girl turned out to be very dramatic as well. I met my next best friend in second grade. We'd pretend to be fairies. But then, whenever I tried to have a "real world" conversation with her, she'd get defensive.

"This is the real world! Can't you see the fairies?" she'd plead.

"Right, yes, they're right there!" I'd say, but I never did see them. "But can we not play fairies for a little bit?"

"It's not playing. They're real. Fairies are real."

I wonder how she's doing now. She also got upset about the same neighborhood girl; I wanted us all to be friends. They didn't like each other. Then Fairy Girl got mad at me, and I went to a different school for a year. Neighborhood Girl was also put into my new school, and our parents often drove us with our siblings. So we stayed pretty close, until her family moved. She took with her a book I had let her borrow; I think she still has it.

In fifth grade, I met a new best friend. I think she was my first girl crush, but I didn't realize it until a few months after we stopped talking altogether. We were friends until sophomore year of high school. We'd gone to the same middle school and high school. Eventually, we joined different friend groups and went our separate ways but stayed friendly; I thought we did. It wasn't until I went to take her to coffee for her birthday that I realized how far apart we had fallen. Her mom threw a surprise birthday party for her. I wasn't invited. She didn't think we were still friends. That hurt. It was truly the beginning of the end.

My most recent ex became my best friend in junior year, but I re-met my current best friend at work and became friends with him again. I talked to my ex all the time; we weren't dating yet. I hadn't come to terms with just how queer I was. We liked each other a lot. Everyone knew too. It was one of those tropes: Person A likes Person B, Person B likes Person A, everyone knows except them. Except then they did know, but they didn't date because Person B's mom thinks Person A turned them gay. Person B's mom cut off contact with Person A. So Person A dates Person C with all these misplaced feelings and confusion, dates Person C just wanting someone to kiss and hold and date. Person A loves Person B. Person A likes Person C a decent amount, but not enough. Once Person B is back on the table as someone to date, Person A considers breaking up with Person C but doesn't so as not to hurt Person C, who they really like and want to see where the relationship is going. Person A considers a polyamorous relationship, never proposes the idea, but never forgets it either. Unfortunately for Person C, Person A is only dating them because they haven't been able to admit to themselves just how queer they are. Dating Person B would also mean closing that chapter on the part of Person A their parents approve of, the straight part, which Person A wasn't ready for.

That's a common trope, isn't it? Is it obvious I'm Person A?

Yes, I did break up with that poor boy (Person C) a week after prom, a whole month after I really wanted to. And though I did really like him, I actually loved Person B. I loved them so much that the earth stopped spinning when they hugged me. It was the safest place I had ever been. With their heartbeat in my ear and their arms around my body, I've never known a sense of security like that. Maybe that's why it hurt so much when they finally walked away. Maybe it was because when I tried to leave for the same reasons a week earlier, they told me we could work it out. I knew we couldn't, but God, I loved them so. I would've given them the world, my heart, my soul, the moon. All they had to do was ask. And they did. And I gave. And I gave, and I gave, and I gave, and I gave until I had nothing left to give. But they kept asking, so I kept giving. What did I give? I'm not sure, but I don't think I've gotten it back—my love, my trust, my soul, my heart. Something has been missing since that terrible day, since they told me they didn't even recognize me. Maybe that's why I haven't been able to forget them. Maybe that's why they're in my head day after day. I'm reminded of them. Maybe that's why I'm still so sad.

--

When I was in fourth grade, I was a wolf girl. I didn't howl at people or bite them or anything like that. I did take the idea of being a lone wolf to a very serious level. I figured I had no friends, even though I had a few. I got really into this book series about a wolf who was purposefully separated from his pack because of a birth defect. He didn't belong. He befriended other various woodland creatures to help him find his family, I think. It was a long time ago, and I'm not sure I entirely remember the premise. I remember thinking I was like that wolf, alone, rejected, looking for my family. No, I had a family. I was being silly. Just because I didn't feel like I belonged with my family doesn't mean they weren't my family. I had yet to learn about "chosen families." I love the idea of a chosen family. I haven't found mine yet.

Losing friends can be just as hard as losing boyfriends or girl-friends, especially when you're not entirely sure what went wrong. Sometimes people just drift apart. Sometimes you get told that one of your friends assaulted your ex-girlfriend, but no one else in the group thinks it's that serious. You don't think he would do something like that, not that you don't believe her, you do, and you cut contact with him. But he was your friend. You trusted him. Then he assaults you. You try to tell your other friends, and they say, "He'd never do that to me. He's made it clear he's not attracted to me like that."

"How fucked up is it that the only reason he can have a normal, respectable friendship with you, is that he isn't attracted to you?" I was basically shouting at them, trying to get them to understand. I got reprimanded for saying that.

I try not to hate people. I feel like it's a waste of time and energy. I don't care for this person, so I'm done with them. It's that simple. I don't need to like everyone, and they don't need to like me. I don't need to hate them either though. I make a conscious effort every day to not hate people. The people who've wronged me, the boy who assaulted me, the boy who catcalled me when I was eleven, the boy who threatened to take his life three times if I didn't date him.

It'd be easy to hate them. They hurt me. They broke me, changed how I interact with people. It's a hole I won't let myself fall into. I don't hate. My best friend thinks one day, I'll just decide that I hate him and don't want to be his friend anymore. We define hate differently. That was a bad argument. I think that's where a lot of disconnect is for me and other people who use the word *hate*. It's so intense for me. It's all encompassing. It's tiresome and active and heavy. For other people, it just means "to severely dislike" something or someone. It's almost passive until they're reminded of the person or thing they hate. I don't understand that. Hate is so strong and aggressive and mad, at least, to me it is. Learning that people don't see the world the same way as I do wasn't a difficult concept to grasp. Learning that words mean different things to different people was a little bit harder to understand.

I remember being told, "I know you said that thing to me to be hateful and mean. I know you. I know you wanted to hurt me."

That wasn't true. I said, "Remember when we made plans to hang out, and then you didn't even text me for three months?" because it was true. You hurt me. We made plans to get together when I was going through a difficult time, and then you ghosted me. How is it hateful to call you out on that? How is that wrong? Maybe I'm too close to it to see how it could affect other people. Maybe she's wrong.

"You're full of hate, and none of your friends actually like you. They all think you're mean and awful and don't want to be friends with you, and just don't know how to tell you."

Hearing those words was my biggest fear realized. None of my friends like me. Ouch. It's almost worse thinking about it now, considering the friends in question don't talk to me anymore. Knowing I made an effort to stay friends, I specifically spoke to them about how, what I did was wrong, and I knew that. I apologized. I wanted to stay friends with them, and I was willing to do whatever I could to prove that. It didn't even matter. It's almost worse than flat-out rejection. Being close with people and then losing them is somehow both better and worse than never being close with anyone at all.

Whenever I feel someone pulling away from me now, I let them. I guess sometimes it's considered ghosting, but they stop responding first. I just never say anything else. I stop putting effort forward. It hurts too much when they still leave, when you plan a surprise date to try to reignite the relationship, complete with kittens, and you still get dumped. You still have to drive them home after they break your heart into a thousand shards.

"You were right. We're too different now. You've changed too much, and I haven't changed at all. You're not the person I fell in love with. I don't recognize this person you've become." My ex was crying. I was crying. How could he say that?

It had been over a year, seventeen months since I asked him to date me.

I wish I had said, "We're supposed to change. I was growing as a person, as a functional adult in society. What were you doing? All this time, what were you doing?"

That was rough. What do you say to that? *Yes, sorry, I'll become the same person I was a year ago, right away, let me unlearn everything from our past year together.* That doesn't make any sense. It still doesn't. It probably never will.

--

I was exposed to the idea of self-harm in middle school. Apparently, everyone knew that horizontal cuts were for attention. Vertical cuts were actually bad, which isn't true at all. All cuts are bad. All forms of self-harm are bad. I didn't like myself, so I began to cut. Not very deep, I didn't like cutting. It hurt. I just thought that's what you're supposed to do when you don't like yourself. I taught myself to hate myself. It was super fucked up.

When I told my friend what I had been doing, I was almost surprised by their reaction. They were scared for me, I think. I told them I would stop. And I sort of did. They cared about me, and that felt amazing. I knew, I knew what I was doing was wrong. I understood why it was wrong. I couldn't help myself. I told someone else. They told me they loved me. I think that was one of the first platonic "I love yous" I ever got. Maybe just the first one I remember. I didn't mean for it to get out of hand, for it to go that far. I stopped cutting, but I kept picking. I told maybe one or two people that picking was my way of self-harm, which is true. I told them I did it because I hated myself, which was only partly true. I told them I wanted to stop, but I needed help, which was truer than I wanted to admit at the time.

I liked a boy. I think. It was almost purely lustful. Lust, for a middle schooler, was like the highest form of love. I wanted him. I needed him. At least I convinced myself I did. I don't know if he ever liked me. But we were friends, and I wanted to keep him as a friend, whatever the cost. I made up a lie, a terrible, terrible lie about some rare illness. I didn't think about the consequences of it, what was going to happen by going through with it. As fucked as it was, I did my due diligence on the lie. Everything about it was fact, except the part where it applied to me. I craved attention; I just didn't know it. When he found out it was a lie, he was pissed. I was pissed.

"Okay, yeah, I lied. I'm sorry. I'm not sick, but I do want to die a little bit." Who doesn't? (Mentally stable people, I guess.)

"What? Do your parents know?"

"No, of course not. I don't want to be another drama they have to deal with." Not wanting to be another drama would lead to me feeling very isolated in future years.

Everyone knows this story. I asked him not to tell my parents. He did anyways. They had a talk with me. I was mad at him; I had no right to be. He did the right thing by sharing his concerns for my safety. Years later, I thanked him. I was in therapy, doing better. I apologized. We never spoke again. Classic. I never told anyone. It's the one thing I'm the most ashamed of. It's the one thing I want to take back.

No one else got a lie like that from me, maybe little white lies, the ones I tell for basically no reason. Maybe I'd be telling a story, and instead of saying, "I went to this thing alone," I would say, "My friends and I had a great time at this thing." Is that pathetic, telling a white lie to make myself seem not as lonely? When I was twelve, I met a boy. He was Trouble, with a capital T. I liked him, a lot, too much maybe. He was tall and had nice hugs, validated me, held my hand, made me laugh. I was infatuated. My friends didn't particularly like him, but they liked how happy he made me. I loved him. I don't know if he ever loved me. The first time we broke up, it was because I didn't want to kiss him yet. I wasn't ready. I had midterms and softball and church things. The pressure to kiss him was just added stress. Yes, I know, lesbian-stereotype alert, softball. Ironically, my first real girl crush was another girl on the team. I agreed to be gay on Tuesdays with her. That might've had something to do with why I wasn't ready to kiss that boy, but I didn't put it together at the time.

Funnily enough, I was happier after we broke up. I had less stress. He wasn't pressuring me anymore. Midterms were over. Life was good again. It took about a week for him to realize I was happier without him. Then he wanted me back. I said no. I didn't want to date someone twice then, and I still don't. I was happy being his friend. That was a good decision on my part. My friends supported it. Then he wrote me a note—the absolute worst note. Apparently, he regretted losing me so fucking much that he wanted to kill himself. He was going to slit his throat in the garage. I remember this plainly.

"As I held the cool steel to my neck, I closed my eyes and thought about you, your smile, your laugh, your body. And it made me want to live. You make me want to live. Please, take me back." What. A. Twat.

I was twelve, maybe just barely thirteen. So was he! Who thinks to do that at twelve years old? Or maybe it was right up my alley? I lied about having a deadly disease. He lied about having deadly thoughts and actions. Maybe we were made for each other. That's not true. Just like that boy I lied to didn't deserve what I did to him. I didn't deserve to have this done to me. I felt like it was my responsibility to save him, I mean, only I could. Nobody else seemed to understand that I was the only one who could fix this. I got back together with him, and we kissed. And it was good, good in the absolute worst way. We continued to write each other notes during that month or so that we were together. During that time, he tried to hang himself and drown himself. I don't remember what kept him alive when he tried to hang himself. I think he just failed, but that note wasn't even to me. Of course, thoughts of me gave him the motivation to not drown.

All my friends I confided in said, "You should know better." How? This had never happened to me before; it has never happened to me again. I was being manipulated. I was the victim. How is it my fault that this happened to me?

Victim-blaming is common in situations like that. When I was walking my dog, I got catcalled. I told my friend, and he asked what I was wearing, nothing very provocative, just a crop top and skinny jeans.

"Well, duh. What did you expect going outside like that?"

When I got assaulted, he put his fingers in me and a noise escaped my lips. "See, you wanted this."

It would be so easy to hate these people. These boys who hurt me. It would be so easy to flip that switch. I don't want to hate people. They make it so hard not to. I'm angry about it, I'm allowed to be. It took me a long time to learn that I'm allowed to be angry about things, and it is so therapeutic to acknowledge and feel the anger. I don't hate though. I stand my ground. They're not worth it.

--

I'm terrible at keeping my own secrets. Other people's secrets are no problem mainly because after a while, I forget them, not all of them but most of them. Also, who cares? I can keep some of my own secrets, like the faking an illness thing, losing my virginity, sending scandalous pictures. Hell, I even hid my sexuality for almost three years. I'm currently hiding my gender identity, or my lack thereof. I suppose my ability to keep a secret depends on how serious I mentally rate it. I'm more likely to tell a secret about something I'm excited about, like a present for a friend, definitely more capable of hiding things that make me look bad to anyone, faking illness. Sometimes, I am a child. I overshare. I get too excited about little things. I giggle at innocent jokes. I miss looking at the world through a child's perspective.

When you're young, the world is so full of wonder and light and excitement. You get a balloon at the store or a party, and your day is made! It's the best thing to ever happen to you! Santa is real. The Easter Bunny leaves you notes! Your elf on the shelf takes your Barbies out for a joy ride! There's magic everywhere, waiting to be found. I believed in Santa until fifth grade, when a classmate was making fun of people who still believed in him. Then I found my parents putting out the Christmas presents, kind of a rude awakening. Sometimes I like to say I believe in Santa; it makes Christmas more fun for me. I think magic is out there as long as you believe it is. Like Tinkerbell, people have to believe in her, or she dies. Magic has to be believed in, or it can never be found.

I miss being a child. I'm just a broke college student, barely holding on, barely making rent. I can't even get gas right now or food. Little kids can't wait to grow up. In some ways, I still can't wait to grow up. Only, "grow up" means "financially stable in my own place" where it used to be "in college with friends!"

God, I miss that optimism. Where did it go? Can I ever get it back?

--

Do you ever think about the people in your life who helped shape you into who you are today? The pieces of your personality you picked up from someone you might not even talk to anymore? How you mirrored the behavior and dialect of the people closest to you so much so that you continue these behaviors after they're no longer in your life, bands you like, food, clothing, hobbies, games, etc.? I love The Beatles, excessively. I think they had a profound impact on music as a whole, that they challenged the society of their time, and it was absolutely worth it. The only reason I started listening to them was because of the crush I had in elementary school. And the only person in the entire world that I'm actually terrified of is the reason I love *Percy Jackson* so much. They were why I began reading it in the first place.

I learned how to solve a Rubik's Cube because of a boyfriend I had in middle school. I can only solve one layer now, but I'm sure the knowledge is somewhere. I sing because my mom sings, and I got a lot of my music taste from her. I rekindled my love of Legos because my current best friend loves them too. I love superheroes because of my dad. I know which pronouns are right because of a video someone made about me using them for me.

Who would I be if these people didn't have such prevalent roles in my life? Even people who I don't really know had a hand in shaping who I am today.

—

Sometimes I have terrible intrusive thoughts, like someone watching me as soon as I close my eyes or someone reaching out to grab me from my back seat. I had that thought the other day driving to school. I thought I saw an arm out of the corner of my eye reaching out to grab me, and I jumped. I turned my head to look behind me and saw nothing. My car doesn't even have a backseat. Still, I terrified myself. Being born female and perceived as a woman has put limits on what I'm able to comfortably do, safely do. Being told from a young age to always make sure someone isn't hiding in my backseat or following me through a store, how to carry my keys to make them also function as a weapon, lock the car as soon as I'm inside, don't go outside at night alone. I'm not sure how much of what I think about daily is preventative safety and how much is paranoia.

I don't give my number out to strangers, and when I answer the phone at work, I don't give my name. Some random guy stopped me the other day and said I was cute. I said thank you and kept on walking. He called after me, asking to exchange numbers. I yelled back that I'm gay. That was the end of that.

I drove to Publix late one night, and a dude in the parking lot was just hanging out. I hadn't brought my phone with me since I was right down the street from my house, and my phone wasn't fully charged. It was June. As I was leaving the store, he walked up to me.

"Hey." He seemed to be in his twenties, blue shorts, gray T-shirt. He didn't look to be dangerous.

I had two options, answer or ignore. I could've ignored him, but he could've gotten violent if I did. He didn't immediately creep me out, so I answered him.

"Hi."

"How you doin' tonight?"

"I'm doing pretty all right." I never stopped walking to my car, nor did I slow my pace. We were alone in the side lot of the store, only the streetlight I was parked under to light the way.

"That's cool, that's cool. You're pretty cute. You got a phone number?"

"Oh, thanks. No, I don't have a phone."

"Oh. What about an e-mail?"

"No, my parents are pretty anti-technology."

"Well, how am I supposed to reach you for a date?"

"I'm actually gay, so you're not." He was following me.

"You're gay? Me too."

"Wow! You're gay too? Well, happy pride month!"

I think he quickly realized what he had just said because he walked away almost immediately after that. I got home safe and told my friends about this so-called funny encounter I just had; I still think it's a little funny. I had to focus on the humor because otherwise I would have been sitting in fear of how poorly that could've gone at any given moment.

I didn't have my phone on me. I told him I didn't have a phone and that my parents weren't big on technology. He could've grabbed me. I could've ignored him from the get-go and pissed him off, causing him to attack me. He could've gotten frustrated with the conversation and decided it was easier to grab me. He could've tried to get into my car as I was getting in and taken me. He could've followed me home and attacked me later. I was really lucky, really fortunate, that these thoughts didn't seem to cross his mind.

Early in one of my relationships, I confessed that it took me a while to feel at ease with my partner. They were taller and stronger than I was and could easily overpower and harm me if they ever decided to. The idea that I didn't feel safe with them hurt them, I think. I told them that I made up contingency plans if I needed to escape them. That might've hurt them even more. I couldn't necessarily overpower them, but if I needed to, I could surprise them and hurt them enough to get away.

I like sitting on the edge of rows or booths, so I'm not trapped by anyone. I keep a close eye on cars following me, from behind me or in front of me—you know, if we're at a stop sign and they put on their blinker after I put on mine to go the same way I indicated, if they slow down when I do to stay close to me, if they've made the same turns I've made for three or more turns, if they turned into my neighborhood, and I didn't recognize the car.

How much is paranoia? How much is justified? Where's the line between the two things? Who decided where to draw it?

--

I've come out of the closet as lesbian, queer, and agender to so many people over the last four years. Sometimes it's easier than other times, like if I know someone will have a positive response to me. I hate coming out, over and over, again and again. It's stressful. It's annoying. It's one of the worst parts about having accepted my sexuality, my queerness. Even if I come out to one person or a small group of people, there's always more, always someone who doesn't know, which isn't exactly something I can be upset about. National Coming Out Day came and went, and I came out again. Everyone pretty much already knew, but I made a post for the few stragglers who didn't.

I didn't have to do that. I don't have to come out, no one does. It's a personal choice naturally. It just feels right to let everyone know. I didn't want to hide anymore. It's exhausting, hiding such a major part of myself, like being forced undercover, having to watch my words and my outfits and my actions and how close me and my friends would sit, lying about an aspect of myself that affects every part of my life. I hate coming out.

--

I think I failed at living. Is that possible? I've replaced real, tangible emotional connections for a strange, hyperfixation on a celebrity whose life I will never affect simply because they won't reject me and hurt me. I suppose I've become terrified of vulnerability. I asked for help; and though I got some, I also got a diagnosis, clinical sadness which, I suppose, is depression. I'm depressed, clinically.

They say God gives their strongest soldiers the biggest battles. I'm not a strong soldier. I'm among the weakest. This isn't a big battle. It's just too big for me. Apparently I'm in a trench. I've climbed out of them before, but this one is deeper and longer and darker and muddy. I can't get a foothold. I can't even stand up. All I can do is army crawl through the dirt and mud and storms, getting scratched by tiny twigs and sharp rocks, leaving my body exposed to all the infections and bacteria that seeks somewhere warm to hide from the rain.

I'm running from something. Rather, I'm crawling from something. I have no idea what. If I lay my head down to rest, it might reach me, and I'm so tired. I have nothing left to give, no energy to continue on. I want to sleep for a long time. I want to sleep and sleep and sleep until my body forgets what it means to be awake, until my brain forgets it ever felt anything but the peace and calm of a dream. I don't want to die; I just need to take an extremely long nap.

I want to be a doctor; I've told that to anyone and everyone who asks. How am I supposed to be a doctor if I can't even get my first degree? My second degree. I have an AA, not a BA. I have nothing left in me to even try to succeed, no motivation, no willpower, no strength. I tried to argue that I can't be depressed. I'm not sad.

I'm simply diminished, empty, barren. Apparently, that's worse than being sad. Who knew?

I don't even have the energy to be properly sad or angry or hurt or anything. I'm just so tired.

--

I realized in the shower this morning that my mind and body decided to give up on my goals, without really letting me know. I've been beating myself up lately about my mental state and ability—or, rather, my lack thereof—without really thinking about why this was happening, the deeper issue, the root of the problem.

It's really easy to look at failure and think negative things about yourself.

I know better than this.

I'm smarter than this.

How could I let this happen?

Maybe I can't do this.

I won't be able to succeed.

I've failed.

It's a dangerous, vicious spiral that can quickly get out of control, snowball if you will. These things get easier to believe the longer the behavior goes unchecked, which is problematic in its own way. Getting help is okay and necessary. Everyone needs a little pick-me-up sometimes. Humans are social creatures, and it's natural for us to depend on one another, to ask for help.

It's hard, almost too difficult, to admit you need help. It's something that I, personally, have praised in others, telling them how strong and courageous and valid they are. "It's okay to not be okay."

Yet for some reason, it feels shameful to admit that I need help, that it's okay to ask. I don't even know where to start, left with only my thoughts as I try to decipher the best course of action to just make it through this year.

It's okay to not be okay.

I can't do my schoolwork. I'm rapidly declining in my abilities to pull myself out of such a dark place.

It's okay to not be okay.

I have the weight of the world on my shoulders, keeping my head down, my back arched.

It's okay to not be okay.

I set impossible goals for myself, overestimating my abilities, and reacting disproportionately when I inevitably can't win.

It's okay to not be okay.

I've reached my breaking point. I'm too far past saving, my education, my relationships are too far gone to fix.

I need help. I'm not okay. I don't know how to be okay again.

If only I knew at the beginning of the semester what I know now, hindsight's a bitch. Would it have really made a difference? I think so. I'm not the best at asking for help, but if I had some insight as to where I'd end up without it, I'd definitely make the effort sooner. I'd shift my weight, raise my head, and ask the nearest person for their hand to pull me off the ground. I'd let people help me take on this insurmountable task. I'd do it differently.

Somehow, somewhere, I got stuck on my poor financial situation, trying to decide between groceries or gas while making minimum wage at a part-time job. It was the only thing I could think about, such a large mountain for such an inexperienced climber. I held on to it, thinking that if I could fix it, everything else would fall into place. And, maybe, there's some truth to that. Unfortunately, this issue has lasted longer than I care to admit. No resolution in sight, and it feels like there is nothing else I can do to fix it, letting the other aspects of my life fall into disarray, too late to salvage.

I suppose this is me asking for help. Who am I asking? I don't know. But I'm asking, and that's already an improvement.

--

I got the opportunity to be a sort of role model for a young girl the other day. I got to know her and some negative experiences she had, being bullied, due to her autism and her queerness. She asked some questions, and I offered support and some answers. I may not have an abundance of friends, but I do know how to navigate dramatic friend groups, which seemed to be her biggest issue. It's strange. My friend brought me over to meet her as an "after" example, after the coming out, after the losing friends, after disagreements with family, after the bad stuff.

It hadn't really occurred to me until then that I've been through so much shit, so much bullshit, and yet I'm still standing. I'm still here. I've come out the other side of it. I'm living in the after.

I think it's strange that, while I've been feeling like my life is simply falling apart at the seams, I am someone my friend looked at as an "it gets better" example—I mean, gee, the proof is in the pudding. I'm living the "better" I've always heard about. I got to be a queer role model for this girl. I got to be the person I needed when I was younger, the person I never got. Is this irony? Is this adulthood?

It was beautiful though. It still is. I mean, I really, it just, it took my breath away to meet her and talk to her and laugh with her. She's so smart and kind and beautiful, and I hope she gets the best life has to offer. What a gorgeous soul.

I hope, one day, I'll see myself as the "after" example that others can see so easily. I can't wait.

--

I take birth control to stop my periods. It's not an unusual reason to take birth control, maybe not the most common—but not unheard of. My periods are the worst. I get cramps and pains and cravings and emotions that make it impossible to think straight. My sex drive becomes aggressively insatiable. I'm hungry all the time for everything and nothing at all. I get irritated and angry and basically just the worst version of myself. Nobody likes me when I get like that.

It's always the worst the three days leading up to the first sign of blood. Never in an obvious way, I can never think about it and realize my period is coming. That probably makes me sound oblivious, I'm not like "Oh no, I'm getting upset more easily than I was yesterday! It must be my period!" It's always more of a slow burn, something like, "These people are so irritating. I had to deal with their shit yesterday, and now again today. I didn't say anything yesterday, but this is too fucking much. I cannot do it."

Then I get mad. I don't yell. I'm not angry, per se, just done, annoyed. It just radiates off me. People notice I'm upset and talk to me gently or ask what's wrong. I respond nicely, politely. They realize I don't want to talk about it and go away, move on. Most of the time, I can analyze things and let them go. But before my period, each time I try to do that, I just get more upset, angrier, this rage bubbling up for three days inside me until I can't do it anymore, and I snap at some poor soul over some little thing that has no significance and probably never will. Then I feel terrible. I apologize. I calm down. I reset. My period comes that same day and stays for a week, a brutal, awful, mind-numbing week, suffering as payment for my inappropriate and disgusting behavior. Then it's gone, forgotten, finally over, until the next month.

Obviously, that's not the worst of it, just the easiest to describe, maybe. In those moments, it's easy to feel like no one understands the debilitating pain or the intense swings from happy to sad to angry to numb. It was nearly impossible to live with. So I live without. I take my tiny pill, and I pray no one decides it shouldn't be free. And I stay happy and calm and in manageable pain in short bursts.

It's good, until I forget about it. Just one pill taken a little too late in the day, and suddenly I'm in fetal position cradling a heating pad and crying until I fall asleep. It's been just longer than twenty-four hours, less than thirty, and it's too late to stop it.

I wish there was an easier way. But this is the only way that works for me. It's the only way I have.

--

I don't think I'm very smart. I'm not stupid. I'm not ignorant or oblivious or just plain dumb. I'm just not that smart. There are people I'm smarter than, and there are people who are smarter than me, which is true for just about everyone. I've always lived a part of my life feeling like I had to prove that I was smart, like if I didn't constantly watch my words and my topics of conversation, no one would believe that I had a working brain in this head.

Around third grade, I was tested for the gifted program at school. I failed. The next year, I was tested again. I passed. The passing grade was accepted over the failing grade, and I was put into the program. And that was it. I was never like the other kids though. I didn't play chess and had no interest in learning. I didn't care about politics or who was in the senate or who was the leader of some random foreign country. None of that mattered to me. None of it affected the life I was living. I only cared about reading books I liked and learning about whatever was being taught to me at the time.

I suppose I was living in a fantasy world of sorts, where I got to focus on the things that felt important to me, and nothing else. I played PC games I liked, read books I liked, watched shows I liked, retained information I liked, talked about things I liked, listened to things I liked. Nothing else really mattered to me, which actually makes sense, of course, since I was only ten. I had no reason to do anything that didn't entertain me in any sort of way.

Chess was something often played by my gifted peers, but it wasn't something I cared about at all. It felt tense, unnecessarily so, like you couldn't just play chess and have fun. No. No, everyone would gather around the game that was closest or lasting the longest and would analyze your moves and the amount of thought that went into each one. At least, that's how it was in the high school gifted classroom. People would always ask me to play, and I would want to try it, to be included. But I would hide behind a thin lie and say I didn't.

"Chess?" I'd say. "Uh, no thanks. Y'all have fun though." I would pretend to be uninterested, as if chess was something I knew how to play but couldn't be bothered to start a game. The words I didn't say, the ones that never left my lips, had more weight to them. *Chess? Sure, but I don't know how to play, and I don't want everyone watching me learn.*

It was embarrassing. It was almost as if everyone else had learned to play chess on their own, with their parents or siblings or friends or online, in preparation for the day that everyone would be playing chess, to get themselves ready for some sort of massive chess showdown. And I was the only one who never got the memo.

There was no way for me to even make up for my lack of chess knowledge. If I didn't want to play chess, there were math equations I could solve, Rubik's Cubes to fiddle with, politics to be discussed. But I didn't want to do any of those. I didn't want to know how to solve a Rubik's Cube. (I had already learned, just forgotten.) I didn't want to do extra math work if I didn't have to. I had my own political beliefs but not a list of cited sources with statistics and facts to back each one up and explain why I was right or even why I wasn't totally wrong.

I quickly learned that to be accepted among these people I considered my friends, I would have to not be like myself. Even that wasn't good enough. Even when I tried, I still failed. I read the major news stories from last night, not this morning—I hadn't checked the updates. I knew the basics of chess, but none of the fancy moves or setups. I could only ever remember how to solve the first two layers of a Rubik's Cube; that last layer will remain forever a mess. I couldn't be myself and succeed. I couldn't be someone else and succeed. I never knew what path to take or which way was right. I tried all the possible outcomes, and I still got it wrong.

It was like constantly being shat on by the universe. "You don't deserve to succeed!" The Universe shouts. "you're nothing.

You're not smart. You're not brave. You don't have friends. You cannot do this. You can't do anything." Yelling. Yelling. Yelling. Yelling. Yelling. Yelling at me to stop trying, yelling at me to give up, yelling at me discouragement and warnings. *I'll never be enough. I'll never be happy. I'll never succeed.*

But succeed I did. I succeeded in school. I made new friends every time I would lose some. I succeeded at work. I fell in love. I found happiness. I was successful, if only for a little while.

I did my best, and it wasn't always enough. And I never felt smart enough, but I did it. I pushed, and I worked, and I learned, and I tried. Average isn't a bad place to be.

They say you never know the "Good Old Days" until they've passed, which is, duh. How can they be the "Good *Old* Days" if they're still going on? Who knows? Maybe one day in the distant future, I'll look back at my life now, sitting at this strange desk, writing nothing to no one on my laptop and think, *Wow. I really had something good going on.* I doubt that though, at least for now.

I don't think my "Good Old Days" are going to be marked by my depressed junior year of college, filled with financial distress and failing classes. Right now, I'm too ashamed to ask for help, too broken to know where to begin the fixing, being told I'm not just depressed, I'm *clinically* depressed, betrayed by my brain, my body, my soul. I'm falling apart at the seams and trying frantically to pull myself back together until I can get to a safe place and sew my rips shut.

Everyone wants their good days to be their young days, their childhood days. Something about graduating college makes people nostalgic for their high school friends. I'm not sure if that makes me unlucky to not have any friends to feel nostalgia for, or maybe it means I'm lucky. I'm not forever wishing to relive days of my youth or connect with old friends. I'm just too unhappy with where I am now.

In all my depressed thoughts, I've never once wished to be taken back to a simpler time. I've only ever longed for the future I can't have yet. I think it's silly. All I wanted to do when I was younger was grow up. For a while, I was happy where I was. I had friends that I loved, a significant other that I adored, goals to achieve. Maybe I longed for naptime and recess, but I was content. Now, I once again find myself wanting to grow up. I just want to grow the fuck up. I want to see myself achieving the things I've set out to achieve. I want those moments to be memories. I want to see a happy and successful person looking at me in the mirror, someone who is smart enough, someone with friends who listen to them, someone who loves themselves more than what should even be possible.

They say your pupils dilate when you look at something you love. I remember the first time I realized my pupils dilated when I looked at myself in the mirror. I cried. They still do, no matter the lighting or any other feelings I'm working through when I look at myself. I understand that to mean that no matter what, at the end of the day, I do love myself. I can find my joy in myself. I'm good enough for me. And that's all I really need.

--

Working in the food service industry has led me to be more sensitive than others to tipping and customer behavior and exactly how busy shit can get out of nowhere. Seeing things from the other side of the magic curtain really did wonders for how I viewed the people working the drive-throughs I would go to. Even if I was in a terrible rush, I would be more considerate and understanding of the people behind the windows. They're just doing a job and getting shit pay. Been there, I get it.

I've always been a generous tipper. Sometimes it's just obvious when someone is overworked and doing their best. Sometimes they could just be having a bad day. Most of the time it's just polite to tip. I remember being at a fast-food restaurant, that had servers, with my dad and brothers, and the waitress was clearly stressed out. She had a lot of tables and lots of people at all the tables—it almost felt wrong to even be there. She kept getting a milkshake wrong, wrong size, wrong toppings, wrong cup. Nothing about the actual quality of the shake, just the presentation, I suppose. My dad said it was a simple task, and when she offered the larger shake for the price of the smaller one, he refused, saying something like he'd "rather get exactly what he paid for." It felt like he was giving her a hard time on purpose, and she was clearly getting frustrated. I felt small, too small to do anything about it, too tiny to tell him to stop, just too small. I did, however, make up an excuse about going back to the empty table for something I forgot. I left the waitress a twenty, as well as a note, apologizing for his behavior.

She was really sweet. He was really mad. And I really didn't care anymore. I had succeeded. She got the tip she deserved, on top of a tip that wasn't nearly good enough.

One time, I went to an ice-cream place with this girl who had come out to me and wanted some advice on how to exist when your parents wouldn't accept you. That was a difficult conversation mainly because I myself was still figuring it out. The lady at the window said my outfit was cute, right as I was paying. I got flustered and told her to keep the change as a tip. It was a four-dollar ice cream, paid for with a twenty dollar bill. She protested, I insisted. In my mind, since she called my outfit cute, she deserved the tip. Logic was not in the building or the brain.

I was more careful after that. I would tip, but only the appropriate amount. I couldn't afford to spend more money in tips than the actual items or services I want/need. Still, I lost money doing that too. The worst was when I was in a drive-through, and I didn't want any coins. So when I paid at the first window, I said "I don't need any change."

He gave me a weird look. That should've been my first clue. He took my cash, put it in the drawer, didn't give me *any* change, and walked away from the window.

He stood there at the drawer for a minute too. I tried to get his attention, but he refused to look at me or just didn't see me. Then he walked off, and I was left wondering how to get my bills back.

At this point, when I'm telling the story to people, I change what actually happened. I tell them that I waited as the car behind me crept closer and closer until the guy came back and asked me what I was doing, at which point I explained what I meant by not needing change, and he fixed the mistake. Or I say that I pulled up to the next window and explained what happened, and they got someone to fix the mistake and give me my change.

In reality, I waited about two minutes; and then I pulled forward, got my food, and left. It was too embarrassing for me to tell people how I actually handled it. I mean, I said I didn't need any change. He was just listening to me, right? I could understand that. I had been confused the first time someone said that to me too. I didn't have a window separating me from the customer, and they explained themselves. And the world moved on. Maybe I was the first person to ask him for no change. If so, then yeah, he did exactly what I asked technically. Realistically, he cost me like thirteen bucks. It's not the biggest deal, just embarrassing. Oh well, what's done is done.

I watch my words. I watch how much I tip. I watch my behavior in a restaurant and everywhere else. I watch it all, like watching myself learn to interact with the world around me, like a kid with money and responsibility. I feel like a kid who pays taxes. It's the worst actually, and I hate it here, in this current life stage, not "hate" hate but definitely having strong feelings of opposition to the life I am currently being forced to live, definitely struggling with it, not having a great time.

--

The other day, I drove to a store across town in search of suspenders for my Halloween costume. I was Jack Dawson from *Titanic*, and it was a great costume. As I drove back to my apartment, I was looking at the roads and the young palm trees that lined them. Palm trees are my favorite kind of tree. I want a small tattoo of one by my ear. Looking at them, I was suddenly overcome with all sorts of emotions and desire that completely overwhelmed me. I forgot where I was and, for a brief moment, imagined that I was driving in California, that I lived in California, in a small one-room house with a kitchen that was so narrow the oven couldn't open completely. There was a kettle and a coffee maker sitting on the top of three shelves that acted as a pantry, a mini fridge, since a normally sized one would never fit in the space, and a small backyard with a tiny patio, surrounded by an impressive array of plants and shrubs. I thought for a second that I had moved there and was going to school there and had a life there. When I remembered myself, where I was and still am, my disappointment was astounding. I wanted to cry, to scream, to just turn toward California and deal with the consequences once I got there.

But I didn't. I couldn't. I knew well enough that I couldn't just pick up my life and take a cross-country road trip with only the money in my wallet and the clothes on my back, even if it was in search of happiness. Instead, I picked up my lunch and drove home, placated with my life but not satisfied with my surroundings.

California, not a perfect state, not by any means. Not necessarily better or worse than where I am now, but for some reason, it's extremely more appealing. Maybe it's just because I went during pride month. Maybe it's just because nothing there reminded me of the life I live or the mistakes I've made. Maybe it's because that one waiter that looked me up and down and addressed me as "buddy," instead of "ma'am" or "sir." Maybe it's because I loved the domesticity of being in that tiny house with someone as we tried our hand at cooking a meal almost from scratch. Maybe it's because the thrill of walking up a mountain was so much more than walking a flat nature trail. Maybe it's because it felt like a fresh start. Maybe it's because it wasn't here.

Whatever the reason, I've never wanted to be anywhere as much as I want to be there. Maybe I just haven't been enough places yet; but for some reason, I have this gut feeling that nothing will be as amazing, nothing will feel so much like home as California will.

--

I think about dropping out of college all the fucking time, for no good reason. It's like, I know I can succeed here if I could get out of my head and just put my money where my mouth is. If I could just get myself to focus, then I could do it. I know I could. I want to do it, pass my classes and learn new things, so fucking bad it's killing me. I want to be good at being a college student. I want to achieve things and become a doctor of Forensic Psychology and go wherever life takes me and make my impression on the world, leave a legacy so I don't fade out and die, die twice—once in reality and once again when everyone who has ever known me (or could remember me) forgets me.

Isn't that just a fucking tragedy? Not only does everyone die. Not only does everyone live their lives knowing one day, they'll be nothing more than dirt or ash or maybe a home to the roots of flowers and trees. In theory, it sounds so nice and peaceful, a life well-lived, and a death proportionate to it.

Someone in South Dakota is getting married, probably, and thinking about how excited they are for their future and how this person that they love is gonna be it for them. For the rest of their lives, they'll be together. Is it strange? Wanting to be bound to someone legally and emotionally and socially for the rest of both of your lives, like a trap that both people want to be locked in? They're getting married, having their first kiss, their first dance, and thinking that they have everything they could ever need in life. And yeah, maybe that's true. Maybe they'll have a family and a house and the white-picket fence almost everyone dreams about. Maybe they'll unintentionally drift apart, losing touch with who they were on that wedding day, losing touch with each other.

I think the worst part has to be the not knowing. You can doubt, and you can cry, and you can scream and yell and kick and fight. You can laugh and kiss and cheer and hug. You can plan and think you have everything down to a science. But you can never know for sure.

Maybe that's pessimistic of me. People fall in love and stay in love all the time, falling more in love with each other every day. It happens all the time. Right now, I don't think it'll happen for me because right now, I'm not sure if I'm capable of falling in love in such an intense way again. I think if I did and it didn't have a happy ending, I'd crumble. It might break me. It took four hours of me just sobbing into my pillow before I told the first person that my heart had been broken, which wasn't just an unwillingness to admit it. I was afraid to admit it. My heart was broken by someone they had never liked in the first place, and I was waiting for the smug but sympathetic "I told you so." I didn't want to hear it. Before I said anything, I gave a disclaimer.

"I know you didn't like them, and I know you're probably happy about this. But I loved them, and I'm in pain. I just need you to be quiet and hug me." God, I had to give a disclaimer before I confided about my heartbreak. Isn't that absurd? Isn't that wrong? Why didn't I feel safe?

--

I don't think I have PTSD. I don't get flashbacks or panic attacks or nightmares. I'm not overly sensitive to external reminders of my trauma. In fact, I'm pretty sure I don't, not from getting held against the wall by my throat, not from getting assaulted in front of my house, not from my car crash that totaled my first car. I think I should have more lingering negative effects from these things than I do. I don't really talk about them, but that's because they suck. No one wants to talk about it. I don't want to talk about it. Whenever I read a story about someone else's sexual assault though, I remember mine. And I learn that they were told the same things I heard, "You had a good time." "You wanted it." "I know you liked it." Those things suck. When I hear or read those things, all I can think is, *See? I knew you wanted it.* That thing sucks more.

I didn't mean to make a noise. It was involuntary. It was, he just, he put his fingers in me, like two or three at the same time, too fast. It hurt. I didn't want it. And when I asked some other guy, let's call him John, why Tim would do something like that, John asked what we'd been talking about before it happened. Tim and I, we were talking about sex. I was thinking about having sex with someone else. Apparently the thought of that was too much for Tim to bear. Upon hearing this, John asked for nudes. I wish I could say I didn't send them, but it was just my boobs. And I didn't care that much. Maybe I should talk about this in therapy. Maybe I should talk about all of it. Maybe I can write it all down and then print these pages and give them to my therapist instead.

I thought Tim was my friend. I trusted him. I thought it was my fault for talking about what I was talking about, for not trying harder to stop him, for making that noise. I know in my head, logically, that it is not my fault. I know that. It doesn't feel like the truth though. I wish it did, but it doesn't. It's like it's true for other people, but not for me. I don't get that luxury, the luxury of not being blamed.

Why do I think like this? How did it get this bad?

--

I don't masturbate. I can't masturbate. I don't want to masturbate.

I don't know which of those statements is actually true. I've done it before, not a lot, but a little bit. Fingering myself to the pleasure of my thoughts or to someone on the phone with me or to very detailed smut. It just never really mattered to me, never got off on it. Maybe I was just bad, needed to practice but lost interest before I really began. My arm got tired. I don't like doing things without knowing completely beforehand what it is I'm going to be doing. Maybe that was some of the apprehension. Is *apprehension* the right word? Lack of desire maybe?

I'm starting to think that I've internalized the church's teachings that masturbation is bad, dirty, sinful, which isn't true. Even the idea that porn is bad isn't entirely reliable. Obviously, it's important to get porn from ethical sites and companies where the workers are treated and paid fairly and have full control in whatever scene they're participating in. Porn and masturbation have always been tied so closely together when the church talks about them. It's almost impossible to believe that one can exist without the other. I remember the main argument against porn being how easy it can be to get addicted to it, which is true of anything that can make the someone feel good. But porn isn't necessarily bad. Masturbation is important for learning about oneself, especially so it can be communicated in sexual encounters.

My overwhelming lack of that self-knowledge is probably why it always kinda hurt, being fingered by other people. I like a little bit of pain, like things a little rough. I'll try almost anything once, except sucking dick. I am still only attracted to women after all. I always thought sex was supposed to hurt. Isn't it supposed to hurt a little bit?

It stopped hurting after a while sometimes. Then the person would like move or something, start the actual fingering after the penetration. When it was gentle, it wasn't that bad. I could focus on being with the person and enjoyed being touched, but when the pressure was more intense, it took longer for me to relax enjoy it.

Have I been forcing myself to have bad sex all this time, just because I think it should hurt a little bit? Damn.

I don't know if that's why I don't masturbate. One thing's for sure: I prefer having someone else touch me. It's more fun. And I really enjoy making someone else writhe with pleasure while I tease the fuck out of them and whisper absolutely nasty things to them. I think that's fun. Knowing I have that power over someone's body, I can influence them in such a major way. It's exhilarating, until they try to act on it. Maybe that's because everyone I've fucked has used or wanted to use a dick. And I don't like dick. That's an interesting thought. I know I've been sexually attracted to some of them. There's no question about that. Maybe I just couldn't get a metaphorical hard-on for a dick.

Did being nonbinary cockblock me before I even knew I was nonbinary? Was it just my attraction to women that limited how attracted I could be to these people who had or wanted male parts?

--

I had my first panic attack in a very long time the other day. I'm not sure what entirely triggered it. Maybe I was just tired. I'd been social all day, and then I had to work until 2:00 a.m. I think my brain was just done for the day, and I still had to push it to do more, to be on for longer. I hate having to be on for the sake of my social relationships. It's absolutely exhausting. I just have to be happy and excited and vibrant and all these things that I just don't always want to be. Why do I feel obligated to do this for other people? Just to be palatable to the majority? It sucks ass, lots and lots of ass.

--

Growing up, as I learned about myself, specifically the things about myself that don't conform to how I was raised and what my parents believe, I began to limit myself so I wouldn't cause problems in my house, my home. I got to be really good friends with the four walls of my room, and I didn't want to leave my bed, not unless I was leaving the house as well. It didn't feel safe, I suppose. I let myself be put into a box, pushed into a corner, and I kept myself there to "keep the peace" within my family. It was terrible. I couldn't really be myself, and I was scared to even really try.

It's Thanksgiving break of 2021, and I'm home for the holidays. It's like I've fallen right back into that same old, dumb routine, which really isn't anyone's fault. My family doesn't know that I'm nonbinary, that my pronouns are they/them, so they don't know not to call me a girl or "she." And it hurts, sure. It feels terrible to be misgendered, discouraging somehow. What hurts more is that it's not something I can be honest with them about. Being kind of a bigot drives that divide between people. One of the worst parts about being queer in a homophobic family is that my family will never know the real me, the me who is loud and proud and excited about dumb things, the me who prefers handsome to beautiful and wants to accidentally be called "sir." They'll never know that about me, and that hurts.

I wish I could tell them. I wish they'd listen to me. Sometimes I want to yell at them, "I'm queer! I'm your child!" and beg them to *look at me* or acknowledge me.

--

The one thing I always forget about until I go home is a huge deal, yet it always escapes me until it's too late. The person who sexually assaulted me lives just down the street. He lives within walking distance of my home, my family knows we aren't friends anymore, but they don't really know why. For the longest time after it happened, I still had to see him in class, see the truck he did it in as it constantly drove past my house. I really thought those feelings would be the worst. I didn't think anything would get worse than seeing him or seeing people sitting in the seat where it happened, not even knowing.

How could they laugh in that seat? How couldn't they feel the terrible air surrounding it? I think it was worse because we were friends. I wasn't expecting it. I was confused when we pulled over, right in front of my house, just out of sight. I laughed when he pushed up my skirt with his hand and met spandex, making some comment about how clearly he wasn't meant to do that, touch me there, since it wasn't easy. But it was easy. I said no, but I couldn't stop him. He was stronger than me. I didn't want to get hurt maybe. I didn't even try harder than telling him no, telling him to stop. For so long, I've believed it's my fault. I know it isn't. I know it's his fault for doing it, for taking advantage of me like that. But it was me who turned him on in the first place, asking him questions about sex I was having, telling my friend stories like I did with my other friends sometimes. Still, they never did what he did to me. Still, I shouldn't have been alone in a car with him. He tried to assault my ex-girl-friend. He grabbed my ass when I was still with her. He shoved his tongue down my throat when I had a crush on him. Why in God's name did I still trust him?

--

It's finals week, the end of my first semester at this really great university, and I still can't make myself get up. I could cry about it, scream at myself until I'm hoarse, absolutely rage and break everything in my immediate vicinity; but I'm just so tired, too tired. I can't get the energy to do anything but pretend I'm functioning normally at work and when I talk to others. I wish I was actually functioning normally; I wish I could pass my classes; I wish my fucking transcript was fully processed so my tuition could be paid, and I could register for classes that I may not even be able to take.

I'm so tired, maybe a little bit angry too. Or maybe I would be if I had the energy to put into being angry. But I don't. So instead, I'm tired, fucking exhausted. I always feel sleep deprived and yet stay awake until the sun comes up, staring at my ceiling, begging for sleep to come, begging to check out of this life that's been beating me down, again and again and again and again. I just want a break, a break that I earned, one that I deserve, one that comes after I've worked my ass off and done all my homework and had the motivation to fucking succeed at something for once. Instead, my winter break will be a stressful one, spent wondering how I'm supposed to get my degree and do all the things I want to do if I can't even push myself to succeed at the things I need to do.

I'm just so tired. I asked for help, and I got it, somewhat. But for some reason, telling my professors I was failing because of depression just felt like an excuse, and a cheap one. It felt like, if I was "exploiting" my depression, then it couldn't be real. Was it?

Depressed people don't advertise that they're depressed. If they do, it's probably for attention. It's like no matter how much I preach mental health and talk about it and say it's normal and okay to be struggling, it never applies to me. I can never connect that last dot.

Sometimes I can when I ask for help. It's why I was able to ask my middle school pastor for help my eighth grade year, but it was also why I didn't think I should see him when he came to visit two years later. I remember thinking how embarrassing it would be. *He'd think I'm so dramatic. He'd be disappointed if he knew I was no better off than I was when he left. I don't want him to see that.*

I think it's why, when I had a panic attack in church and my mom told me it was the Holy Spirit, I was only half mad at her. I mean, what do you even say to that? "Hey Ma, I think I'm having a panic attack in this church pew of a service I didn't want to attend."

"No, you're fine. It's the Holy Spirit washing you of your sins."

My sins? I was gay and anxious and overwhelmed. In that moment, my only sin was not standing up for myself, not whatever self-righteous bullshit she was selling herself 'cause, believe me, I was not fucking buying, not that day or any subsequent ones.

--

I have dating rules.

Never date anyone more than once.

A "break" is just a breakup. Finalize it.

Don't date anyone you see often enough that anything other than an amicable breakup would make day-to-day life unnecessarily difficult. This includes coworkers, classmates, and anyone else who fits the requirements.

I've made these rules as they became relevant, which was in surprisingly quick succession. The first two were made in direct response to one person, the only person in the world I am terrified of. The third I made in response to a situation I faced while working at my first job, and I got the idea for the rule after seeing similar awkwardness unfold on countless television shows.

It's usually never an issue that I have such rules. I only have three, and they aren't the most complicated rules in existence. I hold myself to them as much as I can. It's easy not to break the first two, especially since I'm not currently dating anybody. The last one gives me some pause sometimes, especially if I get a crush on someone I work with, which has only happened once or twice, like I do now which is good fun, I suppose. Really, I want to be friends with her. She seems super cool, but she's also fucking attractive, not to perpetuate the stereotype that people can't be friends with people they're attracted to but damn.

It's a little much to try to handle, which makes it nearly impossible for me to handle it, which makes it impossible for me to have normal conversation with her without blushing like a virgin on prom night. It's less than ideal more so than usual because she's also a tattoo apprentice, and I love tattoos and want so many more than the few I have. This is easily a conversation I could be having with her, except the part where my anxiety and crush make it basically impossible.

To be fair though, she hasn't really tried to talk to me. So maybe I should even out the blame instead of leaving myself as the only one responsible. Or maybe she doesn't even want to talk to me, and I shouldn't think about it nearly as much as I do. Unfortunately, that's way easier said than done for an overthinker with social anxiety.

There's only been one time that I've broken a dating rule. It was a new rule then, to never date anyone more than once, and I was convinced I was in love. So why wouldn't I get back together with someone who said he needed me? Why wouldn't I try to help him? Try to picture it.

You're about to turn thirteen in a few weeks. You've joined the softball team in your last year of middle school. You've made friends on that team, and you finally have an established friend group for the bus ride and lunch. You finally feel like you have a place you belong, people you belong with. Sure, a boy broke your heart a month or two ago, but you're doing so much better now, and it doesn't even matter.

You say you'll always remember him. After all, he was your first love. And when he approaches you, asking you back, you say you'll gladly be his friend, but you don't want to date anyone twice. It's easy to stand your ground at first, and he seems to respect you and your decision. Then you get a note. He asks you not to read it in front of him, says it's serious, concerning but not the end of the world by any means. You can even almost forget about it until you feel it in your pocket when you sit. Then you read the most terrible thing you've ever come across.

> I know you don't want to get back together with me. I don't blame you. I dumped you because I wanted to get back together with [my ex], but when I saw how happy you were, I missed you. I wanted you back. I liked [my ex], but she isn't you, and I broke up with her to try to be with you again. But you rejected me. That hurt a lot.

You finally realized I'm not good enough for you and that you can do so much better than me.

Which is absolutely true now and it definitely was then, but I'm paraphrasing.

I'm a terrible person. I still want to be more than just friends with you. [Blah, blah, blah.] I'm in love with you [here's a country song that can express my feelings better than I can]. Please forgive me.

Last night I tried to kill myself in the garage with a knife. I wanted to slit my throat because I didn't have you, didn't deserve you, so what was the point in living.

This next part should sound familiar.

But, as I held the cool steel to my neck, my brain instantly bombarded me with thoughts of you. Your laugh, your smile, your body. Suddenly, I couldn't bring myself to do it anymore, not knowing I'd never see you again.

They say your life flashes in front of your eyes before you die, well I think the fact that I only thought about you means you're important to me. You brought me back to life, I love you. Please take me back.

Now to you and to present-day me, that reads like obvious manipulation, a full load of crap too big a lie to be true. But when you grew up relatively sheltered with a bleeding heart and a just-re-cently-found-place-in-the-world-you-belong, it reads like a tragedy, Shakespearean-type shit, a romance between two people destined to be together, torn apart by time and circumstance. He said I saved him, and it felt so, so good to be needed like that. I saved his life, with love!

I wasn't fully ready to give in at that point, but he'd worn down my defenses. I wanted to talk to him, make sure he wasn't having those thoughts again and try to get him to talk to somebody. I think that's when I unintentionally gave him his way to get to me. I told him about my own self-harm, how I'd done it, how sometimes I wanted to again, how in some ways I never stopped. I thought it would help him to hear that I understood on some level what he was going through. He hadn't confided in me in vain, hadn't told someone who couldn't possibly relate.

He started to lie about self-harm and being physically harmed by his parents after that. The lies and stories got really, really bad. He started to tell me that not only did he cut (which wasn't a complete lie, he showed me his cut wrists) but that his mom would basically whip him with a belt, that his back was covered in old and new scars from being torn apart by the belt buckle, scars I never saw. He continued to write me notes, and I started writing some back. I think by the time the school year ended, I had around twenty notes from him. He was a really good writer. I was captivated, ingesting his rhetoric with a desperate ache to know him better, to get closer to him, to love him.

We did start to date again. I hadn't been ready to kiss him the first time around, his frustration toward that being part of the reason things ended. However, after reading about how much he loved me, how much he *needed* me, I wanted to be as close to him as I could be. Besides, I was the only one he said he could trust with this shit. He couldn't ask his abusive parents to see a therapist, and if he saw the school counselors, he said he feared that they'd just want to pull them in. I felt I was all he had.

At thirteen years old, I didn't know better. I thought this was love, tragic but pure love. I thought I would marry him. I thought I could see a future with him. I was proud to be the one he chose to confide in. The few friends I told tried to get me to see that he was bad for me, but I was so far gone to him. I thought they just didn't understand us.

"No. We're in *love*. He loves me. I'm helping him. I'm keeping him safe," I'd insist, defensiveness drenching every word. How could they not see it? This relationship was good. I was good for him. He loved me, how could he be bad for me if he loved me?

Someway, somehow, his parents found out what was happening, the lies he was telling. I think they got in contact with my mom and told her so that she could talk to me about it. Two weeks before the school year ended, his parents took him out of school. He wasn't allowed to see me, talk to me, be around me. According to his mom, I was encouraging his negative behaviors. On his last day at school, he signed my yearbook.

I don't remember the entire message, considering I haven't been able to open that yearbook in years now, but the ending stays with me always.

> In four years, when high school is over, I'll find
> you. And if you're dating someone else, well…
> just don't do it.

The end of those four years came and went with no negative consequences save my recent heartbreak. And I moved nearly three hours away from the last place I'd ever seen him, but the fear that he might just turn up one day is excruciating. It probably wouldn't be so terrible if I didn't know that, at least at one point, he would've done it.

About a week after his parents decided he wouldn't go to school anymore, my mom got a call from his mom. He'd run away from home. His mom was upset and demanded to know if I knew anything about it. I didn't. He'd never told me that was something he'd consider. Even with all his negative behaviors that I did unintentionally encourage or enable, I never would've supported him running away from home. All sorts of things could go wrong with that. I was broken then, I think. I called my friend who lived one street over, and we walked all around my neighborhood while I called his friends and asked if they knew anything or had seen him.

After about an hour of crying and pacing and worrying, I got a call from his mom. The police found him walking along some train tracks. Apparently, he was trying to make his way toward me. The guilt and shame I felt was overpowered by the relief that he was okay, but it didn't last long. He lived almost forty-five minutes away by car. Even if he'd made it to my part of town, what were the odds that he'd have actually been able to find me?

I think the fact that he tried, even when the odds were absolutely and completely stacked against him, is what keeps me worried about it now. Even after he apologized two years later, even when he started to try to get back together with me while he had a girlfriend a year after that, even though I haven't seen or heard anything about him since, I have no idea what would happen if I had to be face-to-face with him again. The uncertainty is almost so unbearable that I wish he'd just find me just so I could be over and done with.

Please, God, don't let him find me.

--

I was 16 when I came out as bisexual. I knew I wasn't really bisexual. I knew I was probably a lesbian. But I repressed those feelings in favor of, to put it bluntly, compromising my sexuality to appease my parents. I still liked boys, and I convinced myself I liked them in a romantic way. But I knew I liked girls too. When I finally came out, it was after I had my first girlfriend. Almost a year after we'd broken up, after I'd started to date a new boy (the aforementioned Person C.) I didn't want to lie to my parents anymore, and I tried to be completely honest with them, even while I was lying to myself.

That was my mistake. Without asking my permission, they confided in my youth pastor and the church's main pastor to figure out what to do about me, how to "save" me. While I never had to meet with the church's main pastor, they did rope me into meeting with my youth pastor, who explained that just because I had these "urges" didn't mean I had to act on them. I think this is why so many Christians think of sexuality as a choice. I was told that I had the *choice*—to live how God wanted me to or to live in sin by acting on these temptations.

I was furious and silently seething at what my parents wanted to put me through, at what this man (I was taught to trust) was trying to convince me of. I knew this wasn't a choice. I spent days, weeks, months crying myself to sleep over it, all my internalized homophobia coming to a head in the middle of the night when I caught myself fantasizing about how soft a girl's mouth would feel on mine, how her body would feel wrapped in my arms. It broke me, trying to understand how much I wanted it while hating myself for wanting it at the same time. Why would I choose this pain? Why choose this agony? I repressed the hell out of my feelings. I ignored them completely in hopes they'd disappear. I could still feel attraction to men on some level. Not as a girl, but I didn't know I was anything else yet. I lied to myself and willed myself to be attracted to the boy I was with.

It shouldn't have been so hard. I did still kind of like him. He was attracted to me, so I let him touch me how he wanted. I encouraged it when he got excited, let him get too excited sometimes. He liked it, and I liked him. And I honestly thought that's just the way it worked. Letting your partner get off even if it was doing nothing for you, like you were just a warm body designed entirely for their pleasure. Sometimes he did things to me that felt good. Sometimes he didn't though. For instance, he really liked to slap my boobs, leaving handprints and red marks in a possessive way. It got to the point that before I went on stage in my high school beauty pageant, I didn't let him touch my chest. My dress was low-cut, and any marks would've been painstakingly obvious, especially under a spotlight.

When we broke up after about two months, it was because I knew I couldn't lie anymore. I knew I wasn't bisexual. I knew I only said it to give my parents some sliver of hope that I could end up with a man one day. I knew that was the absolute wrong reason to do so. I knew I wanted to be, though, straight or bisexual. I wanted to like men. I wanted to want to kiss them and date them and marry them. I wanted to not be revolted by the thought of being intimate with one. It was a desire fueled by my own homophobic thoughts, my own hatred for what I was.

I know now that my queerness isn't what I am, rather who I am. It's a part of me. It affects every aspect of my life. I am my queerness as much as my queerness is me. I was so busy trying to please others that I didn't realize until recently that I've long since accepted it. Despite what I've been taught, I chose to love myself.

I remember being in the car with my mom one day talking about homosexuals, explaining how easy I found it to *love the sinner but hate the sin.* "How could you not love them?" I asked. "These people are God's creation, and he loves them. It's our duty to love them as he does."

She was so proud of me for being mature enough to understand that concept. It astounded me that this wasn't a concept that people could easily grasp and understand. People are good. They are kind and nice and caring and gentle. People deserve love. Everyone deserves to be loved. Granted, there are a few exceptions, including violent repeat offenders and those few, genuinely bad people. Generally speaking though, people are good. It's innate in humanity, repressed by the demands of today's society, but ever-present nonetheless.

When I came out as a lesbian, it was over text. At my therapist's advice, I found a day I'd be out of the house for a few hours and sent a lengthy text to my mom. "I like girls. I'm dating that one I keep bringing by the house. We've been dating for a while. I'm not bisexual at all." Then I promptly turned my phone off. The stress was overwhelming. I was at a concert with my friend, Jon Bellion—whose music I adore, determined to have an amazing time. And I did. I was moved to tears when he performed "Stupid Deep." Before that night, it had never been my favorite song of his. But I'm certain it was the overwhelming experience of coming out and then listening to his lyrics.

I felt so unbelievably safe and seen in this moment, by some man on a stage who has no idea that I exist, safer in an open arena—surrounded by strangers, sitting next to a friend I don't talk to anymore—than I had felt anywhere else in my entire life. At the time, it was the safest place I could ever remember being. Now it's just the first time I ever felt safe. I'm fortunate to have since found multiple places where I've felt the safety and comfort I experienced that night. I'm eternally grateful. Unfortunately, those places don't include my childhood home.

Due to a severe thunderstorm warning, the concert ended about an hour earlier than expected. My friend and I stayed with most of the crowd to hear one last song before facing the roads covered with a darkness only a nighttime storm creates. It took longer than usual to get off the island and back home, the main bridge having been closed to traffic. But after damning my phone for beginning to die, our navigation apps lead us to safety. I was so exhausted that the last thing I recall from that night is dropping my friend off and then pulling a shirt on over the rainbow tank top I wore to the concert.

--

I love my car. It's a cute little two-door convertible, manual transmission, love of my life. There's something intimate about the fact that I've paid for this car with some help. I own this car. I've worked on this car's engine. She's mine in every way a car can be. Lately, however, I've been experiencing some issues with her. Like today, for example, she wouldn't start. There wasn't a clicking sound or a weak roar from the engine, just a very high-pitched whine and then nothing.

She doesn't need an oil change. I just got her a new battery less than a month ago. She has new spark plugs. I honestly have no idea what could possibly be wrong. I'm hoping it's an easy fix. I talk to her when I see her or when I'm driving her. I always say hello to her, sing her praises when she pushes ninety on the freeway. I believe that everything does better when receiving praise.

I speak nicely to everything, my car, my succulent, my laptop, my phone, everything. Even when something is upsetting me, I don't raise my voice at it. I tend to go calm and ask nicely for whatever I want or need from it. Of course, that doesn't always work, and I suppose it's more of a correlation than a causation when it does. Nonetheless, it makes me feel better when I ask for something and actually receive it, like asking my car to hold out just a little bit longer so I can get to the mechanic.

It feels disrespectful to be anything other than kind to the things in my life that are making my daily activities possible. Also when the robots take over, I don't really want to be an immediate target.

—

When I was fifteen years old, I went on a date with a boy in a strip mall. We ate at a bagel place and then went into a department store to walk around and talk. Since we were fifteen and in a public place, my parents thought it was fine for the two of us to walk around without a chaperone, not like we could really get up to any shenanigans with an entire crowd around us.

Unfortunately, his parents thought differently, which I learned when his mom called him to ask how it was going and if one of my parents stayed to chaperone. You could hear her yelling through the phone. She was absolutely pissed that no one was there to watch us and not at all shy about making those feelings known. To escape the awkwardness of the situation, I grabbed the first piece of clothing off the rack that I could find and hid in the dressing room for ten minutes. I figured she'd be done by then; ten minutes is a long time to yell at somebody.

I was wrong. When I got out of the dressing room, he held his phone out to me. "She wants to talk to you," he mumbled, staring down at his shoes.

I took the phone and was immediately subjected to the same treatment her son had just received. *You're just fifteen! You need a chaperone! What were your parents thinking?* And so on. When she finally took a breath, I told her that my parents trusted me to be in public with a boy and didn't think a chaperone was necessary for a walk around a store. After five more minutes, she wanted to talk to her son again. A few minutes later, out of the corner of my eye, I saw the boy storm out of the store dramatically. He was my date, so I followed him. I made it outside just in time to watch him *punch the store's concrete wall* in frustration and anger.

We didn't go on another date after that. I don't condone physical aggression, and while I could appreciate that it wasn't directed at me, there's never really a way to guarantee that sort of thing won't happen again. After being lifted off the floor by my throat, I really try to avoid any acts of physical violence.

--

When I was growing up, I loved white roses. They were also my mom's favorite flower. They just seemed so much nicer and softer than red roses. Something about them just felt purer than roses that fell anywhere else on the rainbow, a purer love than red roses, a purer sense of happiness than yellow roses, definitely purer than artificially colored roses. White roses were beautiful.

They still are beautiful, even if I don't like flowers as much these days. It doesn't diminish the natural beauty they hold. Unfortunately, my favorite flower will forever be tainted by the manipulation I experienced at the hands of that boy, that boy who strung me along with threats of suicide if I left, that boy who self-harmed to persuade me into loving him, the one I sometimes wish I had never met but who educated me in unhealthy relationships and dependencies.

He gave me white roses, quoted lines from my favorite songs, ruined things I enjoyed. I used to fall asleep listening to a country music station on the radio. After I was freed of him, after I realized just what he had done to me, I started falling asleep to the sounds, smells, and feel of the night instead, the buzz of the power lines, the wind outside, the air conditioning turning on and off, the weight of my blanket and comfort from my stuffed animals.

Of all the things he took from me and everything he's forever tainted, I miss flowers the most. I want to love flowers. I want to be given flowers by a love interest before we go on a date. I want to look at a vase of flowers on my desk or dresser and be able to enjoy the sight. Whenever I see flowers now, all I can think about is how they're going to die soon. Even though they're beautiful and smell lovely and mean great things, they're going to die; and all those meaningful, hopeful things are going to end with them, which is definitely not what I want to be thinking about.

Recently, I've been more intentional about buying flowers for people I love. Someone was selling them on the side of the road, and I bought two to take home to my mom. When I visited the family I used to babysit for, I bought a small bouquet to give to them. Seeing how receiving flowers brought smiles to their faces just furthered my resolve to fall back in love with flowers, to reclaim that thing that used to bring me so much joy.

I think that's part of what I'm doing by writing, reclaiming my life, bringing joy back into my day-to-day. Sure, I'm depressed. Yes, I'm anxious about a lot of things. And yeah, maybe sometimes it's too much work to even get out of bed in the morning. But by reliving my past and acknowledging how it's lead me to my present, maybe I can start to be excited about my future, excited about all the possibilities.

--

Sometimes, I get bored, ridiculously bored, overwhelmingly bored, desperate for anything outside of my normal, predictable, comfort zone of a life to wake me up from this suffocating nightmare of boredom. I want something to happen. I *need* something to happen, something, anything to just give me a break, to make me feel alive.

At the beginning of my last relationship, we went to a musical. She wore a tie that matched my top and held my hand the entire time. We giggled and whispered and had a wonderful time. I caught an older woman staring at us during the second act, and I smiled and waved at her politely. After intermission, however, both her and the man sitting next to her had left. I don't know for sure if it was directly because of us, but I have a pretty decent suspicion.

It was a magical experience. She opened doors for me, complimented my outfit, held me like she never wanted to let me go. During the year or so that we were together, she would continue to make me feel that way, make me feel loved in a way that no one ever had before. Alas, as all good things do, those feelings ended. We fought more often than we didn't. We left the other feeling unloved and rejected. We fell out of sync and could never quite get back into rhythm. We used our words as weapons, intentionally digging at the other where we knew it would hurt.

God, sometimes I couldn't even stand her, didn't want to look at her. But then she'd text me, or I'd see her in the school hallways. And suddenly it was that first night of love again, holding hands as we walked to a gazebo in the middle of a small park after the musical, laughing as she twirled me once, twice, before holding me and swaying softly to the beat of our hearts. I swear, in that moment, my heart had wings. My soul was laughing. My mind was flooded with endorphins. I felt gorgeous in that moment, being twirled under twinkling lights. I felt loved. I felt happy.

I always used to think that she was my happy ending, that no matter what the world threw at us, we would always have each other. I would never again be bored a day in my life because I had everything I needed with her, losing her felt like my heart literally breaking in two. One minute I was whole, I was happy, I was loved. The next my world had shattered, and my heart was on the floor with boot prints all over it. My happy ending was brutally ripped away from me. Or maybe it was never mine in the first place. It never belonged to me. I never had any claim on it. Seeing as I don't have an ending yet, how can I know it's a happy one? When I get bored, I chase that feeling from the gazebo, the unfiltered joy, the excitement, the love.

One time, I drove my friend across the state to watch the sunset on the Gulf of Mexico. It was beautiful. The sky became a rainbow that was reflected in the ocean. I treasure that memory, hold it dear to my heart.

We ended up going to a beach that every spring breaker had decided to go to, leaving us stuck in bumper-to-bumper traffic for hours on end. It was a shitty day, though. The four-hour drive took nearly six and leaving the top down on my convertible proved to be a disastrous mistake when my friend ended up with a terrible sunburn on one side of his neck.

Going home was almost worse, standstill traffic in the middle of the night. The locals, deciding they had had enough of this, were suddenly making U-turns on a one-way street to escape the chaos. My phone was dying, but we couldn't pull out of traffic unless we never wanted to be let back in. It was 7:00 p.m. when we left the beach and 10:00 p.m. when we left the island and managed to get a phone charger for my car. We were still four hours away from home, which was bad enough. But my wonderful navigation app decided to take us home on state roads instead of major highways to avoid the traffic, leaving me driving through small towns on skimpy roads with no streetlights and no other cars around me. I am 95 percent sure I saw a coyote and the shadow of something bear-like running next to my car for a few seconds.

Around 1:00 a.m., my friend was completely asleep, and I passed a cop that was parked at in a church parking lot. I was already terrified, absolutely shaken to my core because of how dark it was, so I drove like I was taking Driver's Ed. I just wanted to get home, get a few hours of sleep before I worked at 5:00 a.m. The cop car followed me for a few miles, until we get to a stoplight that's literally in the middle of nowhere. I doubt that light gets any traffic when the cop turned from behind me to go a different way. That helped relieve some stress, and before we knew it, I'm walking through my door absolutely exhausted and making a mental note to absolutely never do that again.

The reward was not worth the risk, which is totally fine. There's no way the reward will always be worth it. But half the fun is in figuring that out.

--

I lost my virginity almost unintentionally. One of my friends, whom I love dearly, needed a ride home from work. I offered to pick him up and asked if he'd be able to get some waffles with me before I dropped him at home. We had a super interesting conversation about religion in the car and our relationships with it. Both of us grew up in faith. He was Mormon. I was Baptist. It was a thought-provoking conversation for a couple of sixteen-year-olds.

By the time we got to the restaurant, the conversation had somewhat died off. We began talking about people we liked or were dating. I spoke to him about my fears of my family moving halfway across the country right before my junior year. I wanted to lose my virginity, but not to some basic stranger who I wouldn't really know that well. I think I subconsciously put a lot of pressure on myself to lose my virginity before my senior year. I know there's nothing wrong with waiting until you're ready. I know you absolutely should wait until you're completely ready. I was just sort of forcing myself to be ready for it when I wasn't yet.

When he leaned over to kiss me in the car, I wasn't completely prepared for it. Actually, I wasn't prepared for it at all. He asked if it was okay, and I nodded. When he pushed his hands up under my shirt, I let him. I took it off and leaned my seat back while he palmed at his dick. I let him take off my pants, my underwear. I didn't stop him when he brought his face between my legs. When he sat back up and made a comment about how I really should shave. I shot back with "Well, I wasn't really planning on having sex tonight."

He laughed, and I laughed. And he moved to climb on top of me. In the front seat of a sedan, he climbed on top of me, half naked. I don't remember exactly what happened after that. I know he was *in* me. I know we didn't use protection because neither of us were expecting to need any. I remember that he ended up honking the horn to my car twice with his bare ass. I remember seeing an ad for drinks on the restaurant's window that only said "Thirsty?" And I remember thinking it was hysterical considering what was currently going on.

I remember looking at him and telling him, "I think I'm gay," while he continued to fuck me. I asked him for advice on how to ask out a girl I liked, and he helped me. I don't remember if he finished. I know I didn't finish. I don't remember driving him home, although I know I had to have at some point. I remember that I didn't get my fucking waffles.

Looking back at this interaction, it seemingly lives in a very gray area between consensual and nonconsensual. I don't regret that I lost my virginity to him. I love and trust him to this day. If it had to be with a man, I'm honestly glad it was him, even if it was a very, very strange experience.

His advice worked, and I went on a few dates with that girl. Nothing ever really happened past those few dates though. And I'm still friends with him, although we don't see each other nearly as much as we used to.

--

About two years ago, I applied for an out-of-state internship with a company I really wanted to work for. I'm not entirely sold on working for the same company now, but at that time, it was a really appealing opportunity and I was excited for a chance to participate.

To prepare for two months spent in a different state, far away from home, I decided to take a weekend trip to Savannah, Georgia. I had designed an itinerary for the entire weekend, so I would be distracted from the overwhelming anxiety of being in a new place all alone. While that more or less worked while I was there, it took me over an hour to actually leave my house. I was so nervous I ended up throwing up the amazing breakfast I had made myself before leaving.

Naturally my mom was super concerned for me. She kept reiterating that I had nothing to prove and didn't have to go on this trip at all. I think, at one point, she even offered to reimburse me for everything I paid for in advance. She made some tempting offers, but I wasn't going to give up on myself before I even got anywhere.

She was absolutely right. I had nothing to prove to anyone, except myself. I needed to know that this was something I was capable of. If I was going to get this internship, I needed to be able to be alone in a new city. Savannah, being just a few hours away from my home, was the perfect test city. If anything really terrible happened, not only did I know people in the city, but my parents were more than willing to make the drive to me and help out. My parents are good like that. They really truly care about me and my well-being. I think their homophobia and intolerance is the result of ignorance about the queer community but also because they're convinced I'm going to hell for being queer, which, to them, is the absolute worst thing that can happen to anyone.

So to Savannah I went. I texted my parents when I stopped for gas; and when I arrived at my hotel, I sent them pictures of the room and the view from my window, along with my plan for the day now that I had arrived in the city. I had a tour scheduled at an aquarium of sorts that was technically a marine biology school in the afternoon; and then I was going to see a cabaret in the evening in the Savannah Theatre, a historic landmark near Chippewa Square, after getting dinner in an extremely fancy restaurant that had wine-bottle candle-holders accenting each table.

It was a magical evening and a wonderful experience. I took a trolley tour until I had to leave for the aquarium, which was in a secluded spot and only giving out tours to one party at a time. Basically, I got to spend an hour alone with the pretty tour guide in one of her favorite places listening to her talk to me about all the animals they kept there. She gave me a map that had a little nature trail on it. She told me all the best spots to see the tiny crabs that lived in the surrounding area. I went on this trip about a month after a really terrible breakup. I needed to get out of my head and really put myself in the present. It can be so easy to dissociate and lose yourself to depression if you're not intentional with your actions.

--

What if I just die? What if I just lay down, go to sleep, and never wake up again? What would happen to my succulent? Would my parents take care of it in my absence? Would they let it die because it's too painful to look at it? Would my dog be able to tell that she'll never see me again? Would people I don't like go to my funeral?

I would learn about afterlives. I've always wished that I could learn about the afterlife without dying, which, unless a ghost decides to tell me all about it, is impossible. I wonder if I would be disappointed with what I see. I wonder if I would still experience emotions the same way I do now, if at all.

I don't want to die. I feel like that's important to clarify. I've wanted to before, but not for a very long time. It's just curiosity coupled with a desire to not be in my current situation anymore, which is strange because overall, I'm relatively content with the life I live.

I think it's important to hear from and talk to people who used to be suicidal but aren't anymore, the people who didn't bother planning for their future because they thought they weren't going to have one. I think there's this assumption that they went to therapy and stopped wanting to die and now have their life together, which is odd because no one really has their life completely together.

I think I'm in a weird space mentally. I don't really want to die. I don't really want to exist. The idea of being perceived by other people is unappealing. I'm also sort of lonely, not lonely in a platonic or familial sense, but definitely in a romantic way. I know, I *know*, I'm not in any position to start and maintain a healthy and fulfilling romantic relationship, I'm still working on myself but that doesn't really quell the feelings.

Maybe that's how people find themselves in toxic or unhealthy relationships. Their loneliness is overwhelming for them, making it difficult for them to listen to logic. Or maybe it warps their logic, and they think that finding someone to temporarily get rid of their loneliness is the best thing they could do. Maybe sometimes, it is the best thing they can do, and they fall in love. And they have an amazing and wonderful relationship with someone they really and truly get along with.

I was talking to some of my friends about aromantic people the other day, explaining that they don't feel any romantic attraction for people. My friends immediately started talking about how sad that was, which I completely disagreed with. I mean, first of all, it's a spectrum, like everything is, but they still have those platonic and familial loving relationships. I mean, there are so many different kinds of love. Life can be fantastic and fulfilling without romantic love. I explained that to my friends, and they kind of understood it. But I don't think it really clicked.

Anyways, I would absolutely love to spend a week with a nice girl in a little town in Italy or Spain, maybe Spain solely because I speak a little Spanish, barely enough to get by but enough for maybe a week in the Spanish countryside. I don't want to go to a big city—I mean I do, obviously for the architecture and history and art and everything—but I really, truly, absolutely want to spend at least a week with someone I adore in a European countryside. I want to travel the world. I want to be in love again, even if it doesn't work out. I love being alone and spending time with myself, but I also love being in love and feeling close with someone like that. I miss it.

--

For my eighteenth birthday, I went to the mall with my parents. We ate bad food at the food court, and I built my stuffed bear named Agent B. His only accessory is his fedora.

All of my friends were busy with school activities, whether it was a club meeting or a sports game or practice, and I was given the opportunity to either spend my eighteenth alone or with my parents. Fortunately, I get along well with my parents more often than not, and I was able to have a great time doing silly things.

Unfortunately, by the time my nineteenth birthday rolled around, all my friends who were too busy to celebrate with me the year before were now too busy not being my friends anymore. Birthdays are important to me, whether or not I have anyone to celebrate them with. So to celebrate my birthday, I took myself to a theme park. I got a room at a hotel nearby and arrived a few hours before the check-in time. I was planning on meeting friends who lived in the area; however, one of their roommates got COVID-19, and they were all on quarantine. I spent the afternoon by myself, went on a Ferris wheel, ate some delicious food, and checked in to the hotel where I got an early night in preparation for my birthday the next day.

Despite what people may say, there is nothing wrong with going to a theme park by yourself. Up until I left for the park, my parents were asking me if I was sure I wanted to go alone. They were constantly offering to come with me or coming up with the names of my friends I could ask to go with me. They thought it was sad that I was going by myself, even I started thinking it was a little sad that I had no one I could ask to go with me, when just a few months prior I had friends I thought would always be around. But just like my trip to Savannah, I was determined. I was going by myself. I was going to have an amazing time. I was going to get one of those birthday pins and put it on my shirt because it makes me happy when people tell me "happy birthday" even if I have to tell them to tell me.

There's something therapeutic about going to a theme park by yourself, not having to wait on anyone else, being able to visit the attractions you want on your own schedule, the realization that no one can buy you snacks while you wait in a particularly long line. I think being okay with being alone is really important in life. There's no way to guarantee that someone will always be with you; and in those moments, when all you have is yourself, it's necessary to find that comfort within, to find peace and even happiness within yourself. Some people say that if you can't love yourself, then you can't really love anyone else. That's bullshit. I don't love myself the same way I love other people. There are so many different definitions of love and sometimes people need that help from a loved one so they can learn self-love. I know I wouldn't be where I am without help from others.

Maybe I'm just severely introverted. Maybe it's my social anxiety that's making me biased. I just truly and deeply believe that building a healthy and loving relationship with yourself is key in finding inner peace. Of course, building healthy and loving relationships with other people is just as important, but in such a different way. Standing alone, surrounded by hundreds or thousands of people, and being completely at peace, completely satisfied, is such a freeing feeling. People need people, that's true. Unfortunately, the only person you can never leave behind is yourself. I don't mean to preach self-love or anything. I'm guilty of not always practicing it myself. I just think a lot of people forget the idea behind it. Some people have trouble loving themselves because of their real or perceived flaws. They're not perfect, so they don't deserve love. They build unrealistic and impossible standards and expectations in their heads of what they should be, only to inevitably fall short. They think because of these misgivings, because they weren't good enough, they don't deserve grace or love or happiness.

But self-love shouldn't be through rose-colored glasses. Self-love is flawed. It's imperfect. It's scary. Self-love is looking at yourself, as you are, and saying, "I am good enough. I deserve love. I am worth every effort."

Someone recently asked me how I came to believe these things. I replied that I hit my absolute lowest. I had to get to know myself all over again. But this time, I did it from a place of encouragement and patience.

Self-love is treating yourself to your favorite snack on a bad day. It's seeking out help before burning yourself out. It's deciding to buy food when your depression is so bad you don't have the energy to make any, even though you went grocery shopping a few days before. Self-love is the most intimate, unconditional, personal kind of love that exists. I am good enough.

Self-love is forgiving. It understands that there are good days and bad days. It understands that at any given moment, you are doing the best you can at that time. Sometimes the best you can is getting out of bed for basic hygiene. Sometimes it's cleaning your room or apartment. Self-love gets it.

I deserve love. Self-love is accepting, accepting of all the parts of you that people reject, the queerness that people reject, the religion that people reject, the niche hobbies or interest that people reject. Self-love looks at you, the whole you, and whispers reassurances in your ear when you feel down. I am worth every effort.

Self-love is taking the steps to maintain your health and happiness. It's making the better choice instead of the easier one. It's pushing yourself to hang out with people you love when you want to hide under your blankets. Self-love is hard work, and it isn't always immediately rewarding.

And when it feels too hard or too overwhelming or too uncomfortable to practice self-love, the best advice I can give is to practice self-like and self-tolerance instead. Just be kind and patient with yourself and reconnect with yourself.

--

This may be a biased worldview, considering my own beliefs on the topic; but I have this idea that most people crave something more from their life, something other. I think that everyone, at least once, looks at the life they're living, at the situation they're in, and thinks to themselves that they want something more.

I think some people find it in the form of a significant other or other meaningful relationship, maybe in a job or a new place to live, a religion or certain set of beliefs. I think these things satisfy that craving for more in an obviously realistic and tangible sense. I think some people never find it. They spend their entire life looking for that thing, that *other*, that they see people find elsewhere, and it just never really clicks for them.

I think those people, the ones who never click, I think those people crave something supernatural. I don't necessarily mean witches or fairies or vampires, although those can absolutely be included—I mean tiny magics, paranormal encounters, psychic abilities. I think that's why things like ghost tours and magicians are so popular. My younger sibling even started practicing magic tricks, not witchcraft but card tricks, because they wanted to impress. They felt drawn to it. I think there's magic embedded in the arts, in cooking, in music, in painting, in writing. I think everything created by human hands carry a piece of the Creator's soul within it. I know that I'm trusting you with a piece of mine.

I remember when I went on a trip with my mom to stay in this haunted hotel for a weekend. We stayed for two nights, and on the second day, my dad and older brother came to join us. On the first night, when it was just her and I, we went on this ghost tour that was run out of the hotel. It was a lot of fun, and even though we didn't have any supernatural encounters, we learned a lot about the history of the area we were staying in, which is a bonus with any ghost tour. We had a really fun time, visiting these places after dark, led by a guide with a small flashlight, being told ghost stories and tales of personal experiences other tourists had. We went to a museum, a public park, an old cemetery marker for a cemetery that doesn't exist anymore, and finally ended the tour in the attic of the hotel.

Most of these places were also fun daytime attractions, so when my father and brother joined us the next day, we took them to all the same spots and retold the stories we'd heard, passing on these legends and fables with only our memories to rely on. I was relatively freshly eighteen, so when my dad asked me to take pictures of these places, even though I had pictures from the prior night, I grumbled but complied and forgot about it.

The rest of the weekend went by without any fanfare. A few days after we all got back home my mom asked me to show her some of the pictures I took while we were there. So I scroll through my camera roll and come across this weird picture with a strange circle of light in it. After being confused for a minute or two, I realize what's happened. I must have captured a spirit of some sort on camera. I took two pictures at the old cemetery marker during the day, one right after the other. They have the exact same time stamp and everything. In one picture, there is an orb of floating light, almost like a flashlight being shone directly at the camera. In the other picture, there is a thick wall of vines and leaves that block out most of the sunlight from the same area where the light is coming from. I honestly, truly believe that I captured an actual ghost in that picture.

Now I understand that if you totally and completely think I am lying, and I have absolutely no way to prove to you that I am telling the truth, but I would like you to take comfort in the knowledge that I have absolutely no idea how photoshop works. My family is full of skeptics, and even I am still a little unconvinced about the entire situation, but there is definitely something unexplainable in that picture.

Just the other week actually, I went on a ghost investigation tour with one of my friends. This ghost tour company is also actively "investigating" the different spirits in my city, as well as other cities where the company has set up. Everyone taking the tour got EMF, electric and magnetic field, readers and had the option to walk around with dowsing rods. My friend and I both opted out of the dowsing rods. He thought they looked funny, and I thought they'd be unreliable. But we walked around with our EMF readers held out in front of us looking for any sign of something supernatural.

I later found out, while on the tour no less, that my friend is actually afraid of these kinds of things. He doesn't like ghost tours, and he was hoping not to have any sort of supernatural encounter, which is not why people go on ghost tours. Later on, during the second half of this two-hour tour, we were sitting outside a haunted building, when both of our EMF readers began going off only in the space between us. We both moved our phones out of the way, in case the readers were reacting to them, which did not end up being the case. Naturally, we concluded that the little ghost girl the guide was talking about had decided to join us and sit between me and my friend, so I scooted to the side to make room for her between us. As we walked away, I said goodbye to her but kept my reader around hip level in case she followed us, which she did for about half a block. When it looked like she had finally stopped walking with us, I turned around and waved a final goodbye.

I may not be an active believer in ghosts, but I'll be damned if I don't treat what may or may not be one with respect and manners. I can just imagine being a dick to a ghost I don't believe is real or around and then being followed home and tormented because I pissed it off. No thank you, not at all. I would cry.

Despite my supernatural encounters, I'm still looking for that something more, that something extra to possibly make my life slightly more exciting. I can't wait to find it, but at this point, even if I don't find it, if the universe doesn't decide to hand it to me one day, I think I'll create it myself. Maybe I'm already creating it myself.

I think it's worth asking, can you create your own magic, or do you need to wait to find it naturally?

--

Unfortunately, I've had a lot of morally gray sexual encounters, mostly with boys I've dated or simply messed around with. I'm not blaming them, nor am I blaming myself. No one is really at fault here except the one dude who thought it was okay even as I was saying no. I thought I knew what I wanted at the time, and I thought what society indirectly taught me to want agreed with what I actually wanted. I chalked up any and all hesitation to simply being new at everything, not as apprehension to the task at hand, pun intended. However, because of all of that, when I started dating my first girlfriend, I didn't make any sort of sexual advances on her. I wanted her to feel comfortable enough to initiate any sort of sexual situation, so I only did what I was given explicit consent to do—hold her hand, hug her, kiss her.

There wasn't a lot of open communication in that relationship, and she ended up thinking I was asexual. Naturally, there is nothing wrong with being asexual. There is an issue with assuming someone's sexuality and basing decisions about your relationship on it. I have anxiety, and because of personal experience, I need explicit consent as well as open and honest communication about anything of a sexual nature. I have a fluctuating libido, and I love being able to share desires and needs with someone in that intimate way. I just need to be told it's okay.

Years after my girlfriend and I had broken up, I was diving into information about agender and nonbinary identities and came across a lot of top surgeries. Honestly? It is an extremely exciting idea, definitely very appealing. In middle school, I went from a B cup to a DD, and I've almost always wanted a reduction. Tops don't fit. Dresses that fit everywhere else won't fit my chest. Buttons won't close properly, and people have been sexualizing me before I really understood what was going on. So I held on to the idea of simply chopping my chest off and being done with it. I got binders and tapes. I wore them both unsafely for a little bit, but I did end up deciding I like to breathe easily more than I like being almost flat, which is obviously better than unsafe binding practices. I'm serious. It will always be better to breathe easily and protect your ribs and lungs than it will be to bind for over eight hours a day. Binding for eight hours straight isn't recommended anyways. People tell stories about binding all day, every day for so many years that now they can't bind at all. Even if they get top surgery, they still have back problems or trouble breathing.

I thought about top surgery, but I also thought about how sometimes I really enjoy my boobs. I like having boobs. I like how they feel when they get touched. I like how they look in some tops or dresses. I like them a decent amount of the time. I also love the idea of not having them at all. I would love to go to the beach topless, wear a button-up completely open on a hot day, not have to worry about buying bras anymore. I yearn for those things a decent amount of time as well. My most common feeling about my chest, however, is no feeling. I am completely indifferent to what is or isn't on my chest probably 60 percent of the time, leaving the other two feelings to claim 20 percent each. Top surgery is a huge decision, and at the advice from the Trevor Project's text help line, I started a mood diary for only how I felt about top surgery.

I still absolutely want top surgery, no contest. But I have gained enough insight to see that the $5,000 operation isn't totally worth it. Top surgery is completely different from a haircut. You can shave your head, but at the end of the day, your hair will most likely grow back. You cut off your boobs? They never come back.

Anyways, realizing that I couldn't go through with top surgery, I thought more about my reasonings why, mainly the libido reasons. It wasn't like I masturbated, and I wasn't in a relationship with anyone, so why did that matter to me? After tackling my own thoughts and questions and concerns. I turned to practical research: To figure out how I really felt about the whole topic, I ordered some sex toys online and waited for them to ship because I was way too anxious to go to a store. I was scared and excited, so when they arrived I read every booklet that came with each item.

I thought about exploring my sexuality in a more social manner, but I realized the anxiety of trying to get comfortable, sexually, with someone I didn't actually know overpowered any arousal I might feel. When I thought about touching myself, I basically cringed at the simple idea that I had any genitals at all. I don't want a penis; I don't want a vagina. I simply want nothing which isn't possible, I don't think. Maybe I'll research that next. Anyways, based off the apprehension and, quite frankly, discomfort I felt about my own body, I did look closer at the idea of asexuality, only to almost immediately dismiss it again since I definitely feel sexual attraction. I considered demisexual; but I can, in fact, feel attraction toward people I've never met or talked to. Finally, I settled on the fact that, yes, I am still queer, and I am allosexual, which just means I experience sexual attraction. I am also just extremely anxious and agender.

In an effort to explore my body and understand my feelings, I tried to use a vibrator. I remember liking a small one in the past, so I thought my past experiences with it would make it more comfortable for me now. I don't think I've ever been more incorrect about a topic having to do with my own body in my entire life.

While holding it in front of me, I tried out the different settings, the speed of vibration and the sequences they were in. Then I used the most basic of both, over my underwear even, only to freak the fuck out when my body started tensing and spasming. So of course, I looked it up. I found online discussions where posters felt a similar sense of anxiety and fear when it seemed like they were about to climax. Some comments were helpful and talked about making sure you feel comfortable with who you are with and where you are. Other comments called the poster ridiculous for being afraid of "the best feeling of your life."

One comment talked about something called "orgasm anxiety" and said that it could be the result of any number of things. I turned to the trusty internet to get more information on what exactly orgasm anxiety is, quite literally anxiety and fear about orgasming and what might cause it. Negative sexual experiences were on that list. I clearly am not a professional and did not even realize that people could be scared of orgasming, I've heard that it's supposed to be this wonderful thing, this absolute feeling of bliss and euphoric relaxation. I never once was told that my entire body would spasm and my muscles would tense as the climax builds. I suddenly felt out of touch with my supposed high libido.

I think looking back at my sexual history, it makes sense that I wouldn't be able to use a vibrator without a layer of clothing acting as a barrier or reach climax even though I know I am safe when I am alone in my room. With my own misinformed ideas about what masturbation is paired with every single dubiously consensual sexual encounter I've had, I'm actually rather glad that I discovered this anxiety by myself than with somebody. Of course, the right person won't make you feel embarrassed by it; but I know I still would, especially considering the mental and emotional gymnastics I would've had to do to convince myself I'd be okay with someone touching me where I don't even touch myself.

It's easy to hear people say that sexuality is fluid, even understanding it isn't particularly difficult theoretically. But practically? It's an entirely different ball game. There might be some mixed feelings, some confusing emotions, surrounding topics no one ever bothered to teach, but that's a part of life. I don't need to be ashamed that I have trouble with masturbation or sex in general, even though I have a libido that doesn't always consider my mental blocks. I don't need to be afraid to ask for and have open and honest communication in any relationship, especially when it comes to sexuality, because communication is how you interact with the world around you.

Living in a world that doesn't make room for queer people, BIPOC, disabled people, and basically anyone else who isn't a cisgender, heterosexual white male is hard. Talking about things that others consider inappropriate conversation topics or taboo is hard. Challenging your own perception of the world to understand how others live in it is hard. Learning to love yourself in a world where self-love is seen as selfish is hard. Asking for help is hard.

Forming relationships and connections is such an important part of life, and missing out on these things because it's scary to start a conversation is bound to happen. Don't feel embarrassed when you can't approach that person with the cool outfit, but maybe also put effort toward trying to compliment them the next time you come across them. Most people you see in passing you'll never see again, but if you take that time to compliment someone or smile in their direction, I'm sure they'll remember that good feeling you gave them for the rest of the day.

I know I would.

—

When I was eighteen, I got my first two tattoos. One is a heart on the ankle, that one my parents are privy to; and the other is a small rainbow over my heart, one my parents do not know about. I was super nervous to get my first tattoos, so I took this stuffed wolf with me. I call him my emotional support wolf. Wolves are my favorite animal, so I think it makes perfect sense. When I tell people that I took a stuffed animal with me when I got my first tattoos, one of the first things they ask is how old I was. Apparently, eighteen is too old to need a stuffed animal to keep you company when you get tattoos. Obviously, I disagree.

I think new things and experiences can be scary. It's absolutely acceptable to take whatever steps and tools necessary to make uncomfortable things palatable. I was scared out of my mind. Coronavirus was taken more seriously then, so I couldn't have anyone with me, not that I knew anyone who would want to go anyways. So I did what I needed to do to make sure it was an enjoyable experience. I got my third tattoo done by the same guy. It's my birth chart on my bicep. This time he had his own shop with his wife. Since we already knew each other, it made the whole process a lot easier, even though I was in a part of town I had never been in before. I was older when I got that tattoo and a small smiley face on my finger, my fourth.

The smiley face actually matches a girl that lives in a different city. I drove nearly five hours to go on a date with this girl. She was fantastic. We spent four hours together just talking and hanging out and joked about getting matching tattoos which we did the second time we saw each other. Hers is on her wrist. Sometimes I wonder if she regrets it. I don't. Even if we never cross paths again, I will always have a fond memory of her and our time together. Shit, I might even get it restored if it starts to fade one day.

My fifth and final (as of now) tattoo is a neon T. rex. It's also the colors of the bisexual flag, which would be so awesome if I was bisexual, but I just really love the colors. I have so many more ideas for tattoos that I want, behind my ear, between my shoulder blades on my back, a sleeve on my left arm, etc. I love tattoos. I love what they mean to people. I love how they look. I love how they can express someone's life story with pictures and phrases. I love how it's literally art that has come to life on a person's body.

—

Growing up as a girl influenced the childhood I experienced. I was given a toy kitchen and baby dolls to take care of. My brothers got cars and building blocks and trains. For every *Barbie* I got, my brothers got *Nerf* guns. Every doll for me was matched with something loud and colorful and active for them. Why are outdoor toys gendered? Isn't being healthy and active something to be encouraged in every gender? Even now that I'm agender, being perceived as a woman influences the way people treat me.

When I began babysitting, the little girl I watched had all these baby dolls and princess castles while her brother had video games and remote-controlled cars. Not to say she wasn't perfectly happy with her toys, she's five. If she wasn't happy, everyone would know. It just surprised me how many toys for girls have these undertones of being a caregiver for someone else, how many toys for boys are mainly focused on just having fun or being physically active. I watched this five year-old girl pretend to be a mother to her dolls, to imitate her mommy, while her brother just played video games on his console.

I fully believe that this is what makes it so difficult for women to admit that they don't want kids. It's insane to me. You can say you want to adopt a pet, and everyone starts asking if you're ready for that sort of commitment, if there's enough time in your work schedule to take care of one. But once most women reach a certain age, it's like everyone you know and everyone you don't have all come together to ask why you haven't had kids yet. Why you haven't gotten married to a nice man and started popping out babies, as if there aren't already enough in foster care or orphanages? I don't know why everyone thinks it's their business whether or not someone wants kids. I don't know why so many people feel so entitled to a woman's body that they restrict bodily autonomy for them or ask extremely personal and invasive questions they have no right to ask.

When I was younger, I was sure I wanted kids of my own. I love kids. I love to babysit and watch them for a few hours. I think kids need all sorts of positive influences in their lives, and I love to be able to be one of those influences, even if it's just for a short time. I helped the girl I used to watch get over her fear of monkey bars and those weird curved ladder/stair things enough so that whenever her parents got back home, she would ask me to help her show them what she could do. I made a point to call her fast and strong and smart, as well as beautiful and kind and sweet. If she was having a bad day and needed a break, I let her take a minute and come to me when she was ready to talk about what was upsetting her.

I'm not perfect at watching kids, not by any means. But I know what I wanted at different ages in my life, and I try to be the person I needed. I used to get told I would make a great mom one day, which is a weird thing to say to a minor, but I derived pride from that statement. I was ecstatic to learn that someone thought I'd be amazing at raising kids. I'd think of baby names and whether I wanted boys or girls. I'd watch characters on the television give birth and think that all that pain would be worth it because I'd have a brand-new person that I loved at the end of it.

I'm a little older now, a little bit wiser. I've experienced such intense amounts of pain from periods and cramps, irrational mood swings and all-encompassing cravings. I honestly think, sometimes at least, that if my period pain is any indicator, giving birth would quite literally kill me. That's probably not how it would actually happen, but between not wanting kids and not wanting to experience labor, I will literally never find out.

When I say I don't want kids, people respond with something along the lines of "You're still young. You'll change your mind!" But I already changed my mind, from wanting kids to not wanting kids. I'm not going to change it back and definitely not because some random person thinks having kids is like the only reason to be alive or something. I am twenty years old. I know people who are married and have kids, who are married and don't, who aren't married and have kids, who aren't married and don't. I literally know people in all these different stages of life, people who are happy with where they are, people who aren't, people who want more, people who want less. And there I am, in the middle of it all, with no idea where my life is headed or where I want to end up.

I don't even really know who I am yet. And I'm trying to figure it out, but it just seems kind of overwhelming. Maybe I could handle it if I was just figuring out who I am or if I could focus on where I am in life, but instead I have to think about both of those things at the same time while also trying to learn how to navigate the world most successfully.

—

I love to sing. I sing every single day, in the car, in my room, in the kitchen, in the shower. I just sing all the time. It makes me happy to express myself in that way. I've absolutely always loved to sing. For as long as I can remember, singing has been my thing. Singing brings me joy. For a very long time, I thought I wanted to pursue singing as a professional career choice. I was convinced that I'd be an actor and professional singer. My parents even helped me get headshots and an agent when I was in elementary school, which I am eternally grateful for, even though nothing long term came of it. I was in a commercial or two. My biggest job was a music video when I was ten.

Then middle school started. Because I had the brains and the self-discipline, I applied and got accepted into a magnet program middle school, something generally regarded as a "smart person school." Being in a school that had accelerated courses and held their students to a higher standard pretty much ended my acting career as soon as it started. I look back on those days fondly. My parents have always done their best to be supportive of me and help me achieve my goals, even if they were somewhat untraditional.

Alas, I was again without a creative outlet for all my creative energy, except for singing. I could always come back to singing. And I always have, and I'm sure I always will. In middle school though, I came back to it in a big way. I started singing in the worship band at my church. I had a lot of anxiety about being on stage, but I hadn't completely given up on being a famous singer, so I wanted to get used to it. I can admit now that I joined the praise team with the wrong mindset. I wanted to sing in front of people. I didn't really care what I sang or who I sang in front of. My requirements were a stage I was on, a song I could sing, and people to listen. The longer I was on praise team, the more those desires were being fulfilled, which meant that they would be put to the back of my mind, and I could actually focus on the subject matter in the songs.

As a queer, nonbinary person, what I say next might confuse a lot of people. Queerness and religion don't often blend, but I absolutely consider myself to be religious in a spiritual sense. I believe in God or the idea of an all-mighty Creator. I believe in Jesus. I think he absolutely did exist and was all Creator and all man. I believe he did everything he is said to have done in the Bible. I believe in the Bible, the original translations of the Bible, not the King James Version or "refined" versions of it. I do not think the original Bible said literally anything about homosexuality or transgenderism, just like it says nothing about incest or slavery. Even if it did, in the Old Testament, that's more for history purposes than rules to live by. Jesus, by literally existing, made the Old Testament obsolete. Just like you won't go to heaven for being straight, you won't go to hell for being queer. The only thing that matters for an afterlife in heaven or hell is believing in Jesus and living like he would.

There's a lot of miscommunication over what it means to live like Jesus would. Recently, one of my childhood best friends and I started to have these sort of meetings where we would read a passage in the Bible that talked about the kind of person Jesus was, or is, depending on your beliefs. We've talked about him flipping tables in anger, to cursing fig trees that didn't provide fruit when he was hungry. We've even discussed passages that prophesized his existence and personality. It's been refreshing to hear that my friend and I share such similar views on the idea of Jesus as a person, views that differ or even directly conflict with things we were taught explicitly or implicitly growing up in the same church.

One of the first things we agreed upon was the fact that Jesus was some kind of a socialist. And that, if this man, who so many self-righteous people in this backwater country believe in, were to come back to earth today, he would be welcomed in much the same ways detailed in the Bible, which is to say, not at all. He would criticize God-fearing political leaders for letting people live and die on the streets, for not providing the sick with lifesaving care for free, for judging and hating on minorities and entire groups of people that they don't understand or even try to understand. The image people have of Jesus is a fake and postured image. I can't begin to imagine how many people would be upset simply because he isn't white. In Sunday school and through church sermons, Jesus has been idolized and made out to be this perfect, unachievable standard for what all humans should strive to be.

In an effort to make sure we, as children, understood the weight of his sacrifice on the cross. The adults in our life described him as perfect in ways we could never hope to be, holy in ways our sin makes unavailable to us. He was put on a pedestal and raised above us so high we could never even hope to reach his feet, and we were told to try to be exactly like him since that is what God wants for us. At the same time, we were told that we will never be good enough and the only way to gain entry to heaven is to have Jesus stand in front of us before God and vouch for us, say he knows us because we made the effort to know him. We were filled with awe and wonder, our childish hope and confidence making this impossible standard put upon us seem reachable.

I think, as I got older and was taught more, the way I understood everything shifted from hopeful to hopeless, awe-inspiring to soul crushing. We were taught that God loves us even though we will never be good enough. He loves us not because he ignores our sins, but in spite of them. I think, in a lot of ways, God's never-ending love started to feel like pity love or less important than it was made out to be. Besides, if I can just ask forgiveness for my sins and accept Jesus exists, then where is the boundary? What sins against God can I commit before I die if, on my deathbed, I can repent completely and still be loved and accepted, which, of course, is the entire point. There is no boundary, no limit, no irredeemable act. The underlying truth is that if you do truly believe in Jesus, you will *want* to try to act like him. You will want to treat people kindly and always do your best. You will want to show grace and extend mercy to people who may not deserve it. You'll want to love everyone and everything, you'll be offended by things that hurt others. You'll just want the best for everyone. You'll see a homeless person on the street corner and instead of thinking that it's a scam or that they'll use your $5 for drugs, you'll want to give them what you can because you'll want them to get what they need.

The expectation to act like Jesus isn't this impossible standard that no one can ever meet, this unrelievable pressure to be perfect in everything you say and do. It's simply a plea to be kind, loving and graceful to everyone you meet. And it's really fucked up that, of all the things about religion, specifically Christianity, to be twisted and misconstrued, that this idea to act like Jesus has been so perverted that people think they *are* acting like Jesus by telling queers they're going to hell, by yelling at women walking into reproductive health-care centers, by telling homeless people to get a job to get off the street, by tipping their waiters with Bible passages disguised as fake dollar bills.

It's fucked up that when I sang a religious song in my high school pageant that I fully and truly believed in, as a way of accepting my queerness and my belief system in front of my friends and family, my mom cried. "When I chose that song, *Who You Say I Am*, it wasn't just because it's a great song that compliments my voice," I told her afterward, silently begging her to understand. "It's because I am who God made me to be. All of me was created by him."

"No. It's not," she said through tears, crying over how lost she apparently thought I was. I've taught myself a lot about my own belief system since then. I've focused less on the idea of God or an Almighty Creator and more on Jesus, on who he was when he walked the earth, and on who I want to be while I do the same. By deciding to relearn everything I've been taught about religion, my love for myself grew. My acceptance for who I am grew. My understanding of who I am grew. I have been perfectly and wonderfully made. I have grown and evolved in so many ways. I have faced battles I never thought I could handle. I have climbed mountains that seemed impossible.

I am strong. I am brave. I am loved. I am enough.

--

One summer in middle school, my parents got into an argument with one of my older siblings. I have no idea what it was over or how it escalated so quickly. My father eventually had to step away to work, leaving my mom to wrap up the yelling match best as she could. I hid with my younger siblings in their room, to comfort them and offer what little protection I could. I assumed my older sibling flipped her the middle finger then stalked off to their room based on my mom's final yelled words.

"Do you know what that means?" She yelled toward the hallway. "It means 'fuck you, mom!' That's what you're saying to me!" It was the first time I had ever heard my mother curse, punctuated by my sibling's door slamming shut, and to this day, the only time I've ever heard her say fuck. That seemed to be an end to the argument, this one being one of the worst to happen up to that point in my life. Though based on what immediately followed, I'd have to say it's still the worst argument my family has ever had, the lowest and most unsafe I have ever felt in my own home.

I stayed with my younger siblings, trying to soothe their tears and assure them that the worst was over. This was before I realized how cruel life could be, as my reassurances were immediately contradicted by what sounded suspiciously like my mother pleading for her life. We could hear her sobbing and talking to my older sibling as if trying to calm and soothe a wild animal, trying to reason with them while also trying desperately to get them to stop whatever they were doing.

As it happens, my sibling was holding a dagger to my mother's neck. I am lucky enough to not have been witness to that visually, although as my sibling moved on to yell at my father on his office, I went to collect my mother from the living room, where I found her on the couch, crying into the phone.

"My child just held a dagger to my neck. No, no I'm not hurt. I have other children here. Please send somebody." She was still lying down in the same position I imagine she was forced into, next to a discarded dagger, when I grabbed her arm and gently led her to my younger sibling's room. I remember getting them situated while I listened to my older sibling, one of my best friends and favorite people, yell profanity and berate my father just across the house. I've always been fiercely protective of people I love, and I think this event marks the beginning of that trait.

Once my mother and siblings were busy crying and holding each other, I, in a fit of rage, marched over to the office to yell some sense into my sibling. I mean, seriously, what were they thinking? Threatening *my* mother, making *my* younger siblings so terrified that they were sobbing, putting *my* entire family at risk for what? Homework? Television privileges? I had no idea. So I held my head high, and I went to my sibling. And I absolutely shouted. "What are you doing? These are your parents! They love you! They want the best for you, and here you are throwing it in their faces!" I was shouting at their back at first, as they were focused completely on my father, but I was seeing red at this point. This had gone on long enough, thank you very much. My absolute lack of awareness is most definitely why I didn't see this next part coming. In the blink of the eye, I went from standing in the office doorway to being held against the wall, off the floor, by a hand on my neck. My sibling's hand, not squeezing but not gentle, was wrapped around my neck just minutes after it had held a blade to my mother's throat.

But as quickly as it was there, it was gone. In seconds, my father had left his place behind his desk and had tackled my sibling into a headlock, venom in his words as he told my sibling to never lay a hand on me again. As all this was happening, the police were arriving. I have no recollection of how everything deescalated, but the next thing I remember is my sibling being talked to by one officer in the dining room and another following me and my father to the living room, where my father told the cop that I wasn't afraid of anything, that I stood up to my sibling without a second thought.

"That's extremely brave," the officer said. "I'm afraid of spiders. Doesn't matter how big or small they are." He laughed. Holding his two index fingers just a few inches apart. "They could be this big, and I'd still run, screaming." I laughed at his confession, along with him and my father. The officers eventually left, and just like that, it was over. My sibling was taken off to therapy, which lead to me believe that therapy was the thing that happened when you couldn't handle life by yourself until I started therapy myself. And the incident was never really mentioned again, until maybe about a week later.

My mom and I were heading home after a day of shopping together. We were stopped at a red light when she turned to me and asked me to forgive my older sibling. "They needed professional help," she told me without looking at me. "We didn't know, and you shouldn't blame them for what happened. We all need to forgive them and move on." I nodded politely, but I was upset. Forgive them? They haven't even apologized! I never said another word about the incident and to this day, my sibling hasn't apologized.

Don't misunderstand me. I love my family. I love my siblings and my parents and my pets. I have a relationship with every member of my family, and I hope that isn't something that changes. I hold no resentment toward my older sibling over what happened, and I understand the mental strain and circumstances leading to it. I hold no resentment toward my parents for making everyone move on from the event like it never happened, even though it was definitely the wrong way to handle things. I understand the position they were put in; I understand the desire to get their family back.

One of my therapists explained generational trauma to me like this: my parents can only give as much to me as they were given themselves. My father was shipped off to boarding school in a different country from his family when he was fifteen. After a childhood of being raised by nannies, he wasn't given a lot by his parents. I have a distinct memory of him crying with gratitude and surprise when his father gifted him a car he was no longer using. Even though he tries to do better by us, me and my siblings, he was only given so much.

He was only taught so much. So he can only give us a proportionate amount. My mother witnessed her parents go through a messy divorce. Her mother was vocal about how she felt about everything, but she was also obvious in her vices and thereby putting my mother in between a rock and a hard place. My mom was given more than my father, but not substantially. When she left for college, she had to work through it because her parents were unable to support her financially in any way. She also tries to do her best, but she was only shown, only given so much. And she gives us what she can with what she has, same as my father.

Due to their histories and limitations, my siblings and I have only been given so much. My parents want the best for us. They love us. They want us to be happy. And sometimes their love comes out in ways that hurt, ways that leave us with small traumas, but that is simply the reality of life. Rather than hold a grudge against my parents or my siblings that drives me away from them forever, I've simply decided to show them grace. The world exists in a morally gray area, and you can either reject any sliver of darkness in favor of only seeing yourself in the light, or you can accept that there's darkness in everyone and everything. That darkness doesn't make people terrible or evil. It makes them human, humans who deserve forgiveness and empathy, humans who deserve love.

--

At the age of eighteen, I realized that I wasn't a girl, and I was liberated in a lot of ways. In more ways, however, I was getting increasingly anxious over what my actual gender identity was. If I wasn't a girl, then what was I? How was I supposed to find out? I couldn't talk to my parents about this. All of my friends were cisgender. I even spent therapy sessions explaining the concept of a gender spectrum to my therapist. I had no one to really turn to. Fortunately, I had spent a lot of time on social media posting about and explaining different gender identities, as well as sexualities, so I had some kind of idea about where to look for information.

I started with the identity I knew to be furthest from girl, which, of course, is boy. I toyed around with he/him pronouns. I considered what it might feel like to be perceived as a boy, and I did not care for it at all. I realized I like he/him pronouns only as an accidental misgender, and even though I do prefer being called sir to ma'am, it's really only because I dislike being called ma'am rather than because I like being called sir. I looked into what it meant to be a demi-girl, which is when someone feels like a girl sometimes and like something else other times. That leads me to the conclusion that the times I don't feel like a girl, I also don't feel like anything else.

The more I thought about feeling like a girl, however, the more I realized that no, I really don't feel like a girl. I feel feminine maybe, but I also feel masculine sometimes too. Then sometimes I feel like both like I want to be feminine in a distinctly masculine way or vice versa. I didn't want to be seen as a girl because I was a girl but because I chose to look like one. It was a really weird mental and emotional place to be in. If I'm not a girl and I don't feel like anything else, what am I?

And so I sat down and really thought about what the idea of gender meant to me. What is gender? How does it actually affect my life? How much importance have I given it that it doesn't deserve? I thought about what it means to be feminine in today's society and what it meant in past societies. I considered matriarchal societies and how the women were considered more important because they stayed home and maintained the village while men left for hunts. I looked at the words *boy* and *girl* and asked why people put so much power into these things, why people cared so much about them. I thought about gender reveals, where the fathers get so upset about having a daughter that they act out inappropriately. I thought about the men who weigh in and support those fathers, saying they just want a son to play catch with, as if a daughter couldn't possibly play catch.

I thought a lot about the different kinds of clothing presented to either gender in shops. I thought about how difficult it is for a woman to buy a simple black T-shirt that isn't formfitting or cropped, that has a crewneck instead of a V-neck, that isn't covered in a pattern or slightly translucent. I sat, and I asked myself why.

Why do women need to shave? Why can't men wear makeup normally? Why did I wake up an hour early for school to put on makeup? Why don't I like wearing dresses for important events? Why do I have to? Why do the girls work uniforms look different than the boys?

I looked at all these questions, all these things I had never really questioned before, even if they gave me a moment's hesitation at first, and I realized I couldn't find a good reason for any of them. If women shave for hygiene, then why don't men? If wearing makeup makes a man happy, why can't he wear it normally? As much as I enjoy wearing makeup, I value my sleep more. Why do I feel like I can't go to school without makeup? A lot of women's dresses are short, which can be uncomfortable, so why wouldn't my mom let me get pants unless I had ones with a cute pattern? Why are the women's uniforms so incredibly formfitting? Why do the polos have fake buttons, where the men's polos have real ones? All because society says so?

Imagine if, all that time ago, the word *girl* was given to a young male child, and the word *boy* was given to a young female. Imagine that everything that is traditionally feminine was now masculine, and everything typically associated with masculinity was now a beacon of femininity. The truest form of gender-bending, like "opposite day" for gendered everything.

I imagined those things, and I asked those questions. And I realized that gender means absolutely nothing. I saw this post on social media that basically said to "denounce gender roles but respect gender identity." Everyone is, absolutely, perfectly valid in their gender identities. How people feel is extremely important, and I don't want anyone to think that my way of thinking about gender is invalidating their own experiences with gender and the binary. But this line of thought brought me freedom in an inexplicable way. Suddenly I could do things because I liked them without worrying about how they looked. I chopped off all my hair because I wanted to,.I stopped shaving because I hated doing it. I was able to breathe without worrying about toppling the house of cards that was my gender identity. Although it also brought me a new set of rules I felt I had to follow.

I came across the word *agender*, which just means without gender, and it resonated in an incredible way. I'm not a girl, nor am I a boy, but I'm also not anything else. I'm just me. Why do I have to have a gender to describe that?

In an effort to connect with myself and with the help of internalized misogyny, I ended up rejecting everything feminine, even stuff I enjoyed. I thought to be perceived as truly androgynous. I had to look completely androgynous. I had to wear baggy clothes and have short hair. If I was going to wear makeup, it'd be to look more stereotypically masculine. I thought I had to exist in such a manner that people would try to assume my gender but end up confused instead. And I thought that when people kept using she/her pronouns for me, that I had failed at being agender.

I had to check all the nonbinary, androgynous, no-gender boxes to be taken seriously as an agender person, even though not a lot of people even know that agender is a thing that exists. I put this pressure on myself to fit into stereotypes that I didn't even resonate with in an attempt to be seen as my true self. Some things I found I liked. Other things were just annoying. I liked short hair, even a shaved head, but I also really enjoy long hair. I like baggy clothes and oversized T-shirts, but I also enjoy wearing skinny jeans and tight clothing. I like most sporty activities, and with enough encouragement, want to try almost everything, but I also enjoy lounging with music or baking a cake. But in an effort to be seen, I realized that I was overlooking and rejecting things I loved. I put so much power into other people's perceptions of me that I lost myself somewhere along the way. So I stopped.

Granted this has happened just recently, and it took a long time to be comfortable with it, but I started making a conscious effort to put value in myself instead of in others. I like what I like, and I don't have to be ashamed of it. I like dark colors and light colors. I like wearing makeup, but I don't always want to take the effort to do it. I like dresses and pants. I do not like high heels. I like jewelry. I like earrings sometimes, which is why I stick to magnetic or clip-ons. I don't like having my nails done. I just love myself and everything that means.

Once I started accepting myself as I am, everything else just kind of got better too. I was happier with myself, so I come across as a happier person. I love myself, and I come across as a loving person. There is always room for improvement, and I cannot wait to see where that improvement will lead me because I know that, if at the end of the day, I stayed true to myself and who I am and want to be, that nothing will be too big a challenge or too hard a lesson.

I cannot wait to see the person I become, and even though past me would be extremely confused about present me, she would be proud, the same way I am already proud of future me and all they're going to accomplish.

www.ingramcontent.com/pod-product-compliance
Lightning Source LLC
LaVergne TN
LVHW091202080426
835509LV00006B/785